Dedicated to
all the instructors who strive to improve their teaching

Personality Theories Workbook

FIFTH EDITION

DONNA M. ASHCRAFT
Clarion University of Pennsylvania

Australia • Brazil • Japan • Korea • Mexico • Singapore • Spain • United Kingdom • United States

WADSWORTH
CENGAGE Learning

**Personality Theories Workbook,
Fifth Edition**
Donna M. Ashcraft

Publisher: Linda Schreiber-Ganster

Acquisitions Editor: Timothy Matray

Assistant Editor: Philip A. Hovanessian

Editorial Assistant: Lauren Moody

Content Project Management: PreMediaGlobal

Senior Art Director: Pamela Galbreath

Senior Marketing Manager: Elisabeth Rhoden

Marketing Communications Manager:
Laura Localio

Manufacturing Buyer: Judy Inouye

Production House/Compositor:
PreMediaGlobal

Senior Rights Specialist (Image & Text): Dean
Dauphinais

Compositor: PreMediaGlobal

Cover Image: © Bella D/Shutterstock.com

Cover Designer: Katherine Minerva Grafx

For product information and technology assistance, contact us at
Cengage Learning Customer & Sales Support, 1-800-354-9706

For permission to use material from this text or product,
submit all requests online at **www.cengage.com/permissions**.
Further permissions questions can be emailed to
permissionrequest@cengage.com

Library of Congress Control Number: 2010942662

ISBN-13: 978-1-111-52491-3

ISBN-10: 1-111-52491-2

Wadsworth
20 Davis Drive
Belmont, CA 94002
USA

Cengage Learning is a leading provider of customized learning solutions with office locations around the globe, including Singapore, the United Kingdom, Australia, Mexico, Brazil and Japan. Locate your local office at **international.cengage.com/region**.

Cengage Learning products are represented in Canada by Nelson Education, Ltd.

For your course and learning solutions visit **www.cengage.com**.

Purchase any of our products at your local college store or at our preferred online store **www.cengagebrain.com**.

Instructors: Please visit **login.cengage.com** and log in to access instructor-specific resources.

Printed in the United States of America
1 2 3 4 5 6 7 14 13 12 11 10

Preface

WHY THIS BOOK?

I wrote the first edition of this *Personality Theories Workbook* to provide a resource for instructors of personality courses. As many reviewers of this workbook have noted, many personality theories' instructors want to use case studies, but they have been hampered in their efforts because such cases were not readily available. And while many instructors develop their own cases for use in their courses to demonstrate various concepts, they are limited in the number they can develop because the process is so time-consuming. Some instructors use the biographies of famous people and even their obituaries as case studies to demonstrate points in an effort to develop cases for concrete examples of theory concepts, but famous people are not typical and although their experiences can reflect theory concepts, it is useful for students to have everyday examples of the concepts as well. When I started teaching personality theories classes, I also wanted, and needed, case studies to demonstrate various concepts to make them more concrete, and less abstract, for the students, but I could not find them. I began developing my own cases, starting with only four so that students could practice applying theory concepts. It was redundant for everyone who was teaching a course in personality to be inventing his or her own case studies, so I developed this workbook. And now, instructors of personality classes have over 40 cases to demonstrate concepts!

I firmly believe that, as fellow instructors, we should all share various resources to make our teaching easier and more effective, and that is what this workbook is about. More importantly, I developed this workbook to allow students an opportunity to better learn personality theories and to better understand them by practicing applying the concepts they learned in class or from their texts to behaviors and experiences that could be found in real life. I am happy to say that many other instructors agree with this approach and are utilizing this workbook in their own classes, enough so that I've been given this opportunity to write this fifth edition. Through reading reviews of the previous editions of the *Personality Theories*

Workbook, I was struck by just how concerned instructors in higher education are about their students' learning and by just how widespread this concern is. I am heartened by it and gratified that I can assist in this small way.

Personality Theories Workbook has a mix of case studies that demonstrate both well-adjusted and maladjusted behaviors and theory concepts. This helps students to learn that personality theories are attempts to explain personality in both the normal and abnormal populations. And while many personality theories were developed to explain normal behavior, they did so by studying abnormal populations. Therefore illustrations of both types of behaviors are necessary.

IDEAS ON HOW TO USE THE WORKBOOK

There are a variety of ways *Personality Theories Workbook* can be used to assist student learning. Some of the cases can be used to illustrate points during a lecture. Instructors can either work through the questions with their students or have students work in groups and then report their conclusions back to the class. Other instructors might want students to use the workbook for homework assignments and have them hand in their answers for grading. Still others might use it as a study guide or exam (in-class or take-home). Instructors might also want to use the cases as a basis for students writing application papers. Finally, instructors who want to utilize a constructivist or guided discovery learning approach might want to use the cases as a beginning point for students to develop their own knowledge base.

There are two case studies for each of the major theories in the first section of the workbook. Instructors can decide which of the cases best fits their needs, or they might decide to use both by using one as an in-class example and the other as an assignment. These first section cases are useful in helping students learn and apply theoretical concepts.

There are also two to four questions after each case that allow for theory comparison as students progress through their personality courses. These questions directly ask students to compare and contrast theoretical concepts of various theorists. While using these theory comparison questions initially during the beginning of the course might be difficult, if not impossible, because students have not learned enough theories to compare them, they can be useful later on in the semester, and instructors and students can return to them later. They also can be used later in the ways described above, that is, as take-home exam questions or for the basis of papers.

The second section contains five cases and can be used for theory comparison. The comparison questions in the first section of the workbook are more specific and help students to learn individual theoretical concepts by comparing them to similar concepts from other theories and contrasting them with similar concepts so as to note their differences. The cases in the second section encourage more general theory comparison and demonstrate that the same behavior can be explained in a number of different ways by changing focus. These last cases are great to use at the end of the semester to tie all the course material together and can be used as final exams (take-home or in-class).

ADDITIONAL CASE STUDIES

In this fifth edition I've added two new case studies in order to include examples that demonstrate concepts from Bowlby and Ainsworth's attachment theory. Accompanying these cases are associated application and theory comparison questions. These newly covered concepts are integrated throughout the workbook and are referred to in the theory comparison questions of both the first and second sections of the workbook. Thus, this new edition incorporates a significant number of additional application questions and theory comparison questions.

HELPFUL HINTS AND CONTRIBUTIONS BOXES

In previous editions of the *Personality Theories Workbook*, I introduced Helpful Hints sections for each theorist in order to clarify different terms that different textbook authors use to refer to the same concepts and to assist students in their answering of application questions. In previous editions I also included theory comparison Helpful Hint sections in the second section of the workbook. These allow students to compare similar concepts across the theories. This is useful because some theorists use the same term to refer to different concepts. Others use different terms to refer to similar concepts. In other cases, concepts have similar terms and meanings but still have distinctions. Thus, this new edition includes a Helpful Hints box for Bowlby and Ainsworth's attachment theory and, when applicable, information on attachment theory was included in the theory comparison boxes in the second section of the workbook.

In this fifth edition, additional tools that students can use to help learn the theories have also been included. Boxes explaining the contributions of each theory/ theorist have also been incorporated throughout the first section of the workbook. Students sometimes wonder about the relevance of the material they need to learn. The question, "Why do I need to know this?", frequently is asked, if not verbally, at least in their minds, especially with regards to the older, psychodynamically oriented theories that are not as widely accepted as they once were. Taking time to explain to students why these theories are still pertinent today, and their value as building blocks for more current personality theory building, encourages students to see their significance, thereby helping them to learn and understand those theories.

INSTRUCTORS' MANUAL

Instructors should keep in mind that an accompanying instructors' manual is available to them through their book representatives. This instructor's manual includes answers to each of these questions (which should greatly reduce instructor workload!) as well as other instructional materials.

ACKNOWLEDGMENTS

I must express my gratitude to those who helped me to revise this workbook into a fifth edition. Thanks go to Paul, Sam, Morgan, and Ryan Ashcraft for giving me the time to revise and write this fifth edition. Thanks also to my students who keep me "fresh" as a teacher and who continuously motivate me to improve my teaching. Likewise let me express my gratitude to Clarion University of Pennsylvania, which gave me a summer grant to enable me to make these current revisions. I also appreciate the editorial assistance of Tim Matray and all at Cengage Learning who helped to make this edition possible.

Contents

SECTION II
Additional Theory Comparison:
Multiple Explanations for the Same Behavior

Learning and Applying the Theories

Sigmund Freud (1856–1939)

Psychoanalytic Theory
Why learn this theory?

Contributions

Although a number of aspects of Freud's theory are no longer widely accepted, there are numerous reasons for him to still be considered the "Father of Modern Psychology." Freud was the first to introduce the idea that people might behave in ways of which they are unaware or, at least, that people might be unaware of *why* they engage in certain behaviors. As such, his concept of the unconscious is considered to be one of his most notable contributions to the field of personality psychology and has become a cornerstone of the field that is still very relevant today. Freud's defense mechanisms are also widely accepted as a major contribution to the field of psychology, and many people, even those not in the field, acknowledge them as explanations for behavior. In fact, many other personality theorists later described similar defense mechanisms although they might use different terminology, and some have added to Freud's initial list. Additionally, Freud, through his writings on the psychosexual stages, originated the notion that early childhood experiences affect the development of personality. Although most personality theorists now deemphasize the sexual motivation component of Freud's psychosexual stages, the stages themselves are still widely recognized in the general public, and, even if one does not agree with his interpretation of events at those stages, certainly Freud's observation that those time periods are important cannot be denied.

Case Study 1
Sigmund Freud

It is Friday night. Hank is sitting in his apartment eating a pint of Ben and Jerry's Cherry Garcia ice cream and contemplating this past week, which had been stressful. He is five feet six inches tall and weighs 250 pounds. Today he saw a therapist about his weight for the first time, something he had been considering after yet another woman decided not to continue a relationship with him. After just two dates, Sally told Hank they should not see each other anymore because they were incompatible.

Sally and Hank had met through a chat room espousing the virtues of Macs over PCs, and Hank became impressed with Sally's knowledge of computers and software. After chatting a few times on the computer, Sally and Hank found that they lived in the same city and both were single. Because they seemed to have their love of computers in common, they both thought it would be nice to get to know each other better. They met for drinks at a mutually agreed upon bar and then went on to dinner. The date did not go as well as Sally had hoped, and one could understand Sally's view. She tends to be a calm, friendly person with an aversion to conflict. Hank, however, tends to be quite sarcastic and often says things to others that offend them. For example, Hank made an unkind comment about Sally's occupation. She is an insurance saleswoman, and he implied that she tries to rip off other people by feasting on their insecurities and selling them insurance they do not need. Other examples of his verbal insensitivity include Hank berating the waiter at the restaurant because he was dissatisfied with the service. Hank became so loud that everyone at the restaurant stopped talking to watch Hank and Sally. Sally was mortified.

Far from being occasional, these verbal outbursts seemed to be the norm because Hank engaged in similar behavior on their second date when they went to a computer show. Hank got into an argument with one of the exhibitors about which graphics software package was better.

3

Unfortunately, Hank has always been sarcastic, and his biting comments alienated him from his peers, even as a child. When he was growing up, he had difficulty establishing relationships. Friendships were practically nonexistent for Hank. As a child, while all the other kids were hanging out with their best friends and interacting in groups, Hank was learning to use the computer, which now places him at an advantage in his line of work.

Hank has other annoying habits that tend to alienate others, including Sally. For example, he often chews his fingernails when he is nervous. Although minor, this tendency repulsed Sally. In addition, he is a chain smoker, and Sally is a nonsmoker.

Hank thought that Sally broke up with him because of his weight problem and soothed his ego by telling himself that she was a very shallow person indeed if she could not see past his appearance and value his personality. After all, his weight was probably partly genetic: his whole family was somewhat overweight, including his father, mother, and siblings. He also suggested to others (and to himself) that *he* was about to break up with *her*.

The week after his breakup with Sally, Hank started experiencing chest pains. After a trip to the emergency room, Hank found out that he had a heart condition. The doctor told him that he must stop smoking, lose weight, change his eating habits, and start an exercise program. Otherwise, he was headed for a heart attack that he might not survive. This was certainly good advice. Hank continuously had something in his mouth, either food or cigarettes. He especially ate and smoked a lot when he was nervous. This news about his health was especially disturbing to Hank because he is relatively young. He is a Caucasian man, only 33 years old.

And so Hank was scared into considering seeing a therapist to help him lose weight to improve his health. During his first visit to the therapist, the therapist described himself as psychodynamically oriented and then continued to describe the types of experiences that would occur in the therapy process. Hank felt confidence in his therapist by the end of the session and decided to continue so he would lose weight and become healthier.

Hank also thought about the trying week he had at work. As an employee of an advertising firm, Hank worked primarily with computers. He was the person others went to when they had a computer or software question. A whiz at computer graphics, Hank designed and maintains the firm's Web page. Occasionally, he met with clients or potential clients, but his boss usually assigned this duty to other members of the firm. This week, however, his boss asked Hank to meet with a potential client, primarily because the people who usually did so were too busy working to meet a deadline on a different advertising campaign and because other members of the firm were out with the flu. Apparently, the meeting did not go well because shortly afterward his boss called Hank in and chewed him out, stating that this potential client called Hank a loudmouthed, belligerent cretin. Hank couldn't figure out where this opinion came from; he thought the meeting went pretty well. Sure, he told the client that their health food products were tasteless and that the portions were too small, but the jerk kept self-righteously promoting weight loss and healthy eating. Someone had to put him in his place, Hank thought.

His mother often described Hank in terms that implied that he had been loud even as a baby. His cries used to pierce the air, and his mother would often rush to make a bottle for Hank or give him a cookie to regain some peace and quiet, even when she could not understand why he was hungry because he had eaten so recently. She laughs about it now, but it was stressful at the time.

The ice cream started to make Hank feel better, more relaxed, and once he finished off the pint, he pulled out a cigarette and lit it. The first inhale also helped to reduce the tension he was feeling. He hoped that the next week would be better.

Hank wished that his coworkers would appreciate him and offer him friendship. When he was younger, he thought that by becoming good at computers (which he thought were cool) and being able to answer other people's questions about computers, he would be able to make contact with others and form the close relationships that other people do, but so far, this strategy has been unsuccessful. More than anything, Hank wishes a woman would fall in love with him. He thinks that love will solve all his problems: He would not be lonely anymore, and he would be able to lose weight and quit smoking, too, if he just had the love of a woman.

APPLICATION QUESTIONS

Use Freud's states of consciousness and stages of psychosexual development to help explain Hank's behavior by answering the following questions.

1. What personality (or character) type does Hank display, according to Freudian theory? Provide evidence for your answer. At what stage is Hank fixated, according to the Freudian perspective? Find evidence of fixation in the case study. What would have caused this fixation?

2. Would Freudian theory describe Hank's eating and argumentative behaviors as being internally or externally motivated? Explain the motivation.

3. Find an example of a Freudian defense mechanism that Hank uses in this description. Explain it.

4. Find an example of regression in the case study. Explain it.

5. Would a Freudian therapist view Hank's weight problem as a behavioral problem, in and of itself, or as a symptom of another problem? Explain.

6. What therapeutic techniques would a Freudian therapist, like the one in the case study, likely use? What state of consciousness would be the focus of therapy? How does healing/improvement occur during Freudian therapy?

THEORY COMPARISON QUESTIONS

1. What is an alternate explanation (besides Freud's) to explain Hank's eating and argumentative behaviors?

2. What aspect of Hank's behavior would be the focus of a therapist who is behaviorally oriented? What aspect would be the focus if the therapist were psychodynamically oriented?

3. Use Erikson's concept of lack of intimacy to explain Hank's problems in establishing long-term relationships with women. How does this differ from the Freudian explanation?

Case Study 2
Sigmund Freud

Steve is sitting at a restaurant table waiting for his date to come back from the restroom. As he waits, he imagines what the rest of the evening will be like. The restaurant they are eating at is one of those little Italian places with red-and-white checkered tablecloths and candles in Chianti bottles. A violin player strolls around the tables playing romantic music. Steve considers that these types of restaurants always work well for him. His date would be charmed by the atmosphere and begin to feel romantic. This would allow Steve to make his move, and typically, he and his date would end up at either his apartment or hers for a night of great sex.

Steve is 38, of Italian-American descent, and single: a bachelor by choice, but his friends worry about his happiness. They wonder if Steve is unable to form a long-term relationship, that he has a fear of commitment and an addiction to sex and the passion that marks the beginning of relationships. They also wonder whether Steve's strained relationship with his mother is at least partly to blame for his behavior. Steve's mother, while caring for his physical needs, was not openly affectionate and did not give Steve the demonstrative affection and loving interaction he craved. They wonder if his anger toward her and her negligent behavior toward Steve is being manifested as anger toward women in general.

Steve has been a flirt ever since puberty. In high school, he had a reputation for insincerity. Girls were attracted to him; he was handsome and spent a lot of time and money on his appearance. Unbeknownst to his friends, however, Steve secretly feared that he was unattractive, so he did whatever he could to improve his looks.

The girls he asked out always had a good time on their dates, but it soon became known that he would always pressure his dates for sex and, in many cases, tell them that he loved them to convince them to have sex. He was also rumored to have made one girl pregnant and then claimed that it was not his child. To his close male friends, he said that she was not going to tie him down, that "there were too many women and not enough time." This pattern of relationships continued during college. He would date women, have sex with them a few times, and then break off the relationship. He estimated that by the time he was 21, he had had sex with about eight dozen women. He bragged about this among his male friends.

After college, and through the present time, Steve also continued to form relationships with women that were based on sexual attraction and nothing more substantial. One by one, he watched his male friends settle down and commit to one woman. Every time this happened, he would express astonishment and disbelief, stating that his friends were being duped and that no one would make him live with one woman for the rest of his life. When women agreed to go out with him or go to bed with him, Steve felt attractive, and no one was going to take that away from him. In fact, Steve secretly feared that no woman would find him attractive enough to marry. He believed that these women went out with him initially to get a free meal and would soon want to break up with him when someone better came around. So he broke up with them first.

His friends believed that Steve's latest sexual interest, Diane, would be the one he would marry. She seemed to be all that any man could hope for. She was pretty, smart, caring, and had a good sense of humor. Steve had been dating her for a longer time than he typically dated women, and his friends thought that he was finally growing up and settling down. As it turns out, the relationship lasted longer than usual because she was reluctant to have sex with him. She finally did after a couple of months when she was convinced that Steve really loved her and was not just using her for sex. Unfortunately, Diane should have trusted her initial instincts. Steve broke up with her after they had sex on three different occasions.

His present date was a woman he met at the gym where he worked out. She was very attractive, with a great body. He used to date women he met at work, but after someone accused him of sexual harassment, he decided to no longer date women from work. He was angered by the specific accusation and the hype associated with sexual harassment in general. A man just couldn't follow his instincts anymore without the possibility of losing his job. At least he could still meet women at other places.

APPLICATION QUESTIONS

Use Freud's states of consciousness and stages of psychosexual development to help explain Steve's behavior by answering the following questions.

1. Does the Freudian perspective indicate that Steve's relationships with women are internally or externally motivated? Which system of personality is most involved? How?

2. According to Freudian theory, is Steve aware of why he interacts with women on only a sexual basis? Which state of consciousness is most involved in controlling this behavior?

3. What type of Freudian psychic energy motivates Steve's relationships with women?

4. Which of Freud's personality types does Steve display? Provide evidence for your answer. What would have caused it?

5. At what Freudian stage is Steve fixated? Provide evidence for your answer. Describe the stage and how it contributed to the fixation. What would have caused this fixation?

6. Others might express their behavior differently than Steve if they were fixated at the same stage. Give some examples of how they might behave.

THEORY COMPARISON QUESTIONS

1. How could Fromm's relatedness need explain Steve's relationships with women? How does this compare with the Freudian explanation?

2. How could Horney's concept of basic anxiety explain Steve's relationships with women?

3. How does Melanie Klein's conceptualization of the Oedipus complex differ from that of Freud? Do these distinctions make a difference in explaining Steve's relationships with women? If so, how?

4. Use May's types of love to describe the types of relationships with women that Steve typically establishes.

Helpful Hints

Are you having a problem answering some of the application questions for Case 1 or 2? See if the following will help you.

Freud believed that there were three systems of personality: the id, ego, and superego. The id tells us what we *want* to do; the ego tells us what we *can* do; and the superego tells us what we *should* do. We develop personality during our first six years of development as we progress through psychosexual stages where our libido (or sexual energy) is cathected (attached) to a different part of the body at each of the five stages. We can become fixated (stuck) at a certain stage of development if we have not successfully resolved a conflict that occurred at that stage. This typically occurs because of neglect or overindulgence (i.e., frustration or over-gratification). People who are fixated at a particular stage sometimes develop a personality type based upon characteristics of that stage. When we are fixated and experience stress, we are more likely to regress (or return to an earlier stage of development). We then act in a way typical of that stage at which we are fixated.

Carl Jung (1875–1961)

Analytic Theory
Why learn this theory?

Contributions

While many who have studied Jung immediately think of archetypes, they are not his most important contribution to the field of personality psychology. Instead, Jung's most outstanding contribution to psychology is probably his discussion of his eight personality types. In particular, Jung's concepts of introversion and extraversion are especially valuable, and similar concepts can be found in other personality theories. Hans Eysenck and, more recently, McCrae and Costa discussed ideas similar to Jung's introversion and extraversion. Additionally, Jung's discussion of his functions (thinking, feeling, intuiting, and sensing) are also very significant and are key components in the widely used Myers-Briggs Type Indicator (MBTI), a popular personality assessment instrument. In fact, the MBTI is used in a large variety of applications including assisting people in their career choice and identifying learning styles of students.

Jung was one of the first theorists to take a holistic approach to understanding personality. Thus, although his analytic theory is considered psychodynamic, Jung also contributed to humanistic thought. In fact, Jung's view of psychological health was based on the assumption that people need to become aware of, and integrate, all aspects of their personality, even their limitations. This notion, which he referred to as self-realization, encouraged people to become psychologically well-rounded individuals. For example, Jung's theory is among the first in androgyny speculation. Androgyny means that someone has extensive amounts of both masculine and feminine personality characteristics. The androgynous person, therefore, can act in either traditionally masculine or feminine ways depending upon what the situation calls for. Jung encouraged men to become aware of their feminine side (the anima) and for women to become aware of their masculine side (the animus). In sum, he encouraged balance and growth in his clients, a humanistic endeavor that helped clients move toward completion.

Finally, in his writings on the stages of personality development, Jung also contributed to the view that personality developed throughout life and was not fixed necessarily in early childhood, as Freud suggested. This lifespan approach to development allowed such concepts as the "midlife" crisis to be discussed. In fact, Jung's discussions on the experiences of older adults contributed to the development of the field of gerontology and addressed a population that, up until then, had been neglected in the literature.

Case Study 3
Carl Jung

For lack of a better term, we can describe Bob as a fortune teller of sorts, a mystic. He is 56, with an Irish-American ancestry and accent, and earns his living by telling people what they can expect to happen in the future. He accomplishes this by reading tarot cards and by laying his hands on his clients. He claims to "sense" things when he does this; he can see what will happen to his client. He does not understand how it happens, but he says he can almost see things in his mind's eye.

He also earns money by contacting people who "have crossed over to the other world." In other words, he claims to be able to talk with the dead. To do this, he must be able to have contact with an article that the deceased had touched. Bob explains that it is not the feel of the object that is important in this feat or in predicting the future; rather, it is being able to experience a person's "psychic energy." After touching the object, he concentrates and goes into a type of trance in which he allegedly makes contact with, and talks to, the deceased. His clients believe he is actually doing this and so does Bob. His clients claim that he tells them things only their deceased loved ones would know.

Bob says that he has always had these types of abilities. As a teenager, he says that he would frequently sense that a particular event would occur, or he would know that something had happened even though no one had told him. The experiences involved both minor and more major events. For example, when he was younger, Bob says that he would know when to put the coffee on for his father, who worked irregular hours. Bob just knew when his father was coming home, and his father always wanted a cup of coffee when he got home. Bob tells a story about his grandfather dying: On that day Bob had been filled with a sense of foreboding. Only later that day did Bob learn about his grandfather's death, which explained his sense of dread. Bob firmly believes these memories to be true. Others, however, are more skeptical, believing that he is reinterpreting past memories according to more current beliefs and experiences. For example, even though Bob believes that he has always had these psychic experiences, he wasn't always as interested in the paranormal as he is today. This interest, though always present, really did not expand and encompass his life until he reached the age of 40. It was then that he started having seizures or, at least, he started noticing the seizures. When Bob started having these seizures, he went to a doctor and was diagnosed with simple absence seizures. People who have this type of seizure are not always aware that they've had a seizure because they tend to continue whatever behavior was interrupted by the seizure itself once it is over. During these seizures, Bob simply stares forward. The seizures typically do not last long—about 10 to 20 seconds—and begin and end abruptly. However, Bob knows when the seizure is about to occur because he experiences what has been termed an aura, sensations that indicate the onset of a seizure. For Bob, this includes a change in body temperature and an increase in a feeling of anxiety or tension. It is during this time that Bob claims to be able to see the future or make contact with the dead. Most people who experience these types of seizures do so only during childhood, and the seizures tend to disappear by adulthood. But Bob's started, or he first noticed them, during adulthood, and he takes them as a sign of his special abilities. His seizures can be controlled with medication but the medication causes him headaches and an upset stomach. Beyond this, Bob is reluctant to take the medication because he is afraid that he will lose some of his psychic ability if he controls his seizures. So he does not take his prescription.

As he neared his 40th birthday, and started having (noticing) seizures, Bob contemplated death and began to study paranormal activities. This study influenced the interpretation of his own physical experiences with seizures and, he believes, allowed him to hone his mystical skills, which in turn gradually led to his current occupation and lifestyle.

Today, Bob earns money speaking to groups of interested parties about the paranormal. At these events, he describes his experiences and his beliefs about the "other world." He especially enjoys this type of interaction. It makes him feel knowledgeable and sage, as though he were a prophet and the members of his audience were his disciples. His last speaking engagement drew a crowd of 1200 at a college in California. During this "performance," he singled out a number of people and spoke directly to them, apparently giving them messages from deceased loved ones. Stopping in the middle of his talk because of a seizure, he then pointed to one young woman in the audience and told her that her father had a message for her, that he "understands and forgives." She broke down in tears. He told another woman that her deceased husband wanted to let her know that he was happy.

His friends describe Bob as impractical. Although he has been able to make a living this way, Bob has trouble with everyday tasks: keeping house, keeping track of his money, having enough food. His house is always messy; he needs an accountant to keep track of his money; and he often goes to the refrigerator or cupboard only to find nothing substantial to eat.

His lifestyle is decidedly different from most people's. Certainly, it resembles that of a rock star more than that of a banker, with all his traveling and his "performances." Even when he is at home for an extended period, he has many more visitors than most people have because of personal appointments with him for "advice" and guidance. At these sessions he uses his mystical tools and powers to give his clients information from "the other side." Not surprisingly, his friends consider him somewhat odd and eccentric. Other people who do not know Bob very well think that he is either "wacko" or a con artist. Even his agent/manager thinks of him as only entertainment. Although Bob occasionally is concerned that he is "selling out," he believes that he is helping others.

APPLICATION QUESTIONS

Using Jung's theoretical concepts and stages, assess Bob's personality by answering the following questions.

1. What is Bob's attitude according to Jungian theory? Provide evidence for your answer.

2. What is Bob's superior function according to Jungian theory? Provide evidence for your answer.

3. What are archetypes? In what level of consciousness are they contained, according to Jung's theory? What archetype has Bob been influenced by? Provide evidence for your answer. How does it influence his behavior?

4. At what stage is Bob presently, according to Jungian theory? What types of events should he be experiencing at this stage? Is there evidence for these experiences in the case study? Explain.

THEORY COMPARISON QUESTIONS

1. At what stage of development would Erikson place Bob? Why? How do Erikson's psychosocial stages differ from Jung's stages of development?

2. How could Fromm's concept of the existential dilemmas explain Bob's experiences with mysticism? Compare this concept with Jung's archetypes.

Case Study 4
Carl Jung

Mark is a 28-year-old African-American firefighter who loves his job. Although it does not pay as well as he would like and the hours are irregular, he finds it a rewarding and thrilling occupation. As he attempts to describe why he likes his job so much, his face transforms. It lights up. He looks as if he is reliving the excitement of the latest event to which his fire company had been called. He explains that when the alarm sounds, adrenaline rushes into his system and his body springs to life. He states that when he is on a call, he does not really feel fear, but rather caution—and he feels alive. When he sees the brightness of the fire and feels the heat from the flames, he functions almost automatically, performing his duties bravely but not carelessly. The sight and feel of the blaze and the rawness of his lungs from occasionally breathing in smoke make him aware of his mortality and make him appreciate life.

Part of Mark's job also consists of giving talks to elementary school children about fire hazards and fire safety. He discusses how fires start and grow. He discusses what children should do if a fire breaks out. When he gives these talks, the children look up to him and see him as a brave man, which makes him feel good. He also enjoys the status associated with being a firefighter. The people he helps reward him with praise and thanks. They, like the school children, make him feel important and courageous.

Mark's job is very stimulating. Even as a child, Mark was always seeking out high levels of stimulation. When he was very young, he was always making noise, either talking or singing continuously or trying to make music with things such as sticks and pots and pans. Sometimes he would claim that it "was just too quiet." Favorite games were exciting also. Frequently, he would play games in which he was some kind of superhero. He would be the sheriff who captured the bank robbers, the police officer who threw the bad guys in jail, or the captain who outwitted the pirates (and often it was his little sister who was the bad guy or the pirate or the bank robber).

As a teenager and young adult, he always knew he would go into some type of "service" occupation like firefighting or police duty, and he actually attended the police academy for a short time before deciding that it was not for him. He was concerned that the job would turn out to be monotonous rather than stimulating because of the amount of paperwork and the continuous driving involved in patrols. After his experience with police work, Mark decided on becoming a firefighter because he found it more exciting. This decision was a difficult one for him because his parents disapproved of his career choice. They were concerned about Mark getting hurt or killed. They also disliked the idea of him moving out of their house to go to the fire training academy. Nevertheless, he made his decision and stayed with it. He performed very well at the academy and rented his own apartment for the times he would not be living at the fire station.

Mark's friends describe him as outgoing and happy. He loves life and lives it to its fullest. He isn't an introspective person but he is very realistic and pragmatic. His firefighting colleagues describe him as very competent, always able to adapt rescue techniques to the situation as necessary. He is even quite good at fixing and making things. He likes the feel of working with tools and the smell of newly cut wood. Recently, in his free time he renovated the kitchen of the firehouse.

APPLICATION QUESTIONS

Using Jung's theoretical concepts and stages, assess Mark's personality by answering the following questions.

1.   What is Mark's attitude, according to Jungian theory? Provide evidence for your answer.

2.   What is Mark's superior function, according to Jungian theory? Provide evidence for your answer.

3.   According to Jung's theory, what archetype has Mark been influenced by? How do you know this? How does it influence his behavior? Is Mark aware of its influence? Explain.

4.   At what stage is Mark presently, according to Jung's theory? Specify substage, if appropriate. What types of events should be occurring at this stage?

5.   At what stage, in Jungian theory, was Mark when he was pretending to be a superhero? Specify substage if appropriate.

THEORY COMPARISON QUESTIONS

1.   Use another theory, besides Jung's, to explain Mark's career choice.

2.   How could environmental factors, such as reinforcement and punishment, explain Mark's career choice? What are some reinforcements that encourage

this behavior? How is the focus of this explanation different than that of Jung's theory in explaining Mark's career choice?

3. How could Eysenck's concept of extraversion explain Mark's career choice? What other behaviors could this concept explain?

Helpful Hints

Are you having a problem answering some of the application questions for Case 3 or 4? See if the following will help you.

Many of the theorists you are learning about used terms in a way that is different from today's usage. Jung, for example, used the term *attitude* to refer to an inclination to act in a certain characteristic way: introverted or extraverted. And although introverted today means somewhat quiet or shy, Jung described introversion as a turning inward of psychic energy, an orientation toward the subjective. Likewise, although extraversion today means outgoing, Jung described it as a turning outward of psychic energy, an orientation toward the objective. Relatedly, Jung thought that personality was also composed of *functions* (ways of interpreting the world) in addition to attitudes, and

the terms he used for these functions can still be found in today's language usage, but some have different meanings than what is implied today. The *superior function* is the strongest, the one that we use the most because we are most comfortable with it. The superior function is chosen from among two rational functions (thinking or feeling) or two irrational functions (sensing or intuiting). Thinking is logical activity; feeling is the process of evaluating the world (*not* an emotional response). Sensing involves interpreting the world through the senses (*not* a clairvoyant experience); intuiting is interpreting the world in ways that we are not aware, in ways beyond the working of the consciousness. Combining the two attitudes with each of the four possible superior functions results in eight possible orientations or personality types.

Erik Erikson (1902–1994)

Psychosocial Theory
Why learn this theory?

Contributions

Erik Erikson's eight stages of psychosocial development are his most significant contributions to the field of psychology. While Erikson emphasized the lifespan development of personality, his early stages especially are significant because they can be seen as a guide for parents. For example, during the first stage, where the crisis is one of trust versus mistrust, Erikson discussed the importance of parents fulfilling the needs of the infant so that the child develops a sense of hope that future needs will also be met. In this stage the infant determines whether his/her caregivers are dependable and trustworthy; this can serve as a basis for future relationships, as noted by object theorists and, more recently, attachment theorists.

Similarly, Erikson notes the important role parents play in developing a child's sense of competence and confidence in his fourth psychosocial stage, where the crisis of industry versus inferiority needs to be resolved. During this stage children begin to compare themselves to other children, especially in the school setting. A child can potentially notice that they compare unfavorably with other children: they might notice that they are not as smart, not as attractive, not as athletic as other children. If the child focuses on the ways that they do not measure up, s/he can develop feelings of inferiority and incompetence. Erikson thought that it is the parents' job to help the child feel competent in some other way. Thus, the implications of Erikson's psychosocial stages have had a significant impact on developing successful parenting strategies.

These two examples demonstrate the impact of Erikson's writings on childhood issues but Erikson had an even greater influence on understanding adolescent development. Most notably he discussed the importance of teenagers developing a sense of identity and the fact that if parents push their children to conform to what they want them to be, their own child's identity will not develop. Instead, role confusion will develop, and acting out can occur in response to this confusion. In fact, Erikson blamed adolescent acting out on poor parenting. Although other psychosocial stages are not mentioned here, their worth should not be underestimated. Erikson's theory added to the understanding of personality development throughout the lifespan.

Case Study 5
Erik Erikson

Chrystell is a happy eight-year-old who is just finishing the third grade. Like most parents, Chrystell's were worried about how she would react to school and how others would respond to her. They were especially concerned because they and Chrystell are of African-American heritage and Chrystell would be attending a primarily Caucasian school. They need not have worried. She is doing well. The other children like her, and she has made many friends. She is succeeding academically, not only fulfilling the curriculum objectives, but also surpassing them. For example, Chrystell began learning to read in kindergarten, an activity that usually does not begin until the first grade. Part of the reason that Chrystell does so well in school is because Chrystell's parents are quick to praise her scholastic efforts and help her with schoolwork if she has difficulty.

It seems as though Chrystell has always been easy to take care of. When she was a baby, her mother nursed her on demand and found that Chrystell really did not demand to be fed that often. In fact, there were many times that her mother offered the baby her breast because she felt it had been too long since Chrystell had last eaten. Even after waking up in the morning, Chrystell did not cry hysterically for food. Her mother really did not even feel as exhausted by the newborn as she had been with her other children because she was able to get six hours of sleep starting fairly soon after Chrystell was born. Nighttime feedings came only once each night and Chrystell didn't take very long to nurse; her mother was even able to fall asleep while Chrystell was feeding. When the mother woke up, she would put Chrystell back in the crib, return to her own bed, and fall asleep again herself.

Potty training was not terribly stressful either. Neither Chrystell's mother nor her father felt that they should rush their children into potty training. They believed the kids would eventually learn control and that it was the parents' role to introduce the idea of using the potty to the children and to encourage them, but not force them, into using it if they were not ready. Chrystell's parents tried not to embarrass her when she had accidents; instead, they reminded her to try to remember to use the potty the next time. This approach worked for Chrystell: she learned to use the potty when she was about two and a half years old without much hassle.

Chrystell's parents took this approach for helping her, and their other children, to reach other milestones as well. They encouraged their children to do things like walk, hold a spoon, and feed themselves. They tried to make those activities easier for their children to learn by practicing the activities with them, showing them how to do something, and, sometimes, buying things such as curved spoons, which made it easier to learn to get the spoon to the mouth without dumping its contents. Chrystell's parents tried not to hurry their children into learning these activities, although sometimes it was difficult not to. If an activity seemed too difficult, most of the time they would put it aside for a short while and try it again later with Chrystell or her siblings.

As Chrystell got older, her parents tried not to dictate her play activities. Instead, they gave her a couple of choices and let her choose which she preferred. Many times her parents did not need to even do this because often Chrystell would just go off on her own and amuse herself. Sometimes she would just look at pictures in books. At other times, she would play with her dolls. At still other times, she would play with her Legos®.

The only time Chrystell's parents could remember having trouble with her was when her little sister was born. Chrystell's younger sister was a demanding baby and had been born through Caesarean section, so her mother had been limited physically in what she could do with Chrystell and in the time she could spend with her. Chrystell tried to express affection toward the baby but sometimes would hug her too hard. Chrystell's mother was not sure whether this was done on purpose or not. She thought that Chrystell was jealous of the baby because she would say things like, "You always hold the baby, Mommy." Chrystell also started to stutter. Chrystell's mom would try to reassure her by saying things like, "I know you feel like the baby gets more attention than you but I held you this much when you were a baby too." Her mom tried to be understanding of Chrystell's jealousy and did not try to make Chrystell feel bad about it. When her mother was finally feeling better, the baby was less demanding, and her mother was able to spend more time with Chrystell. The stuttering eventually went away, and Chrystell became gentler with the baby. Now as this school year ends, Chrystell's mother hopes that the rest of her school experiences go just as well and that her influence will continue to guide Chrystell's development positively.

APPLICATION QUESTIONS

Using Erikson's psychosocial stages of development (especially the first through the fourth) analyze Chrystell's life by answering the following questions.

1. What is the crisis experienced in Erikson's first stage of psychosocial development? How did Chrystell resolve this stage? What was the outcome of the crisis? Was it favorable or unfavorable?

2. What is the crisis experienced in Erikson's second stage of psychosocial development? How did Chrystell resolve this stage? What was the outcome of the crisis? Was it favorable or unfavorable?

3. What is the crisis experienced in Erikson's third stage of psychosocial development? How did Chrystell resolve this stage? What was the outcome of the crisis? Was it favorable or unfavorable?

4. What is the crisis experienced in Erikson's fourth stage of psychosocial development? How did Chrystell resolve this stage? What was the outcome of the crisis? Was it favorable or unfavorable?

5. Erikson's theory is sometimes described as a good guide for parents. Find examples of this guidance in the case study and describe them.

THEORY COMPARISON QUESTIONS

1. How could Maslow's theory explain Chrystell's experiences? Are all her needs fulfilled? Explain. How do Maslow's needs compare with the crises in Erikson's stages?

2. Use Bandura's concept of reciprocal determinism to explain how Chrystell's stuttering was resolved after her baby sister was born. How is Bandura's theory different from Erikson's in its emphasis?

3. How could Sullivan's good mother/bad mother personification explain Chrystell's breastfeeding experiences? How is the emphasis of Sullivan's theory similar to that of Erikson's?

4. How does Erikson's concept of initiative compare with Rotter's concept of locus of control?

Case Study 6
Erik Erikson

B etty, Caucasian and now 68, contemplates her life. She sent her children off to college and eventually saw them fall in love, get married, and start families of their own. She should be happy, but she is not. Instead, she feels dissatisfied and wonders if her life would be better if she divorced her husband of more than 40 years. She would like to do so but lacks the confidence to carry out this drastic change. She doesn't believe she could live on her own. She always had someone to take care of her: first her parents, then her husband. Now she doesn't believe that she could support herself financially.

Betty's childhood was fairly uneventful. She was the second of two children; her brother is three years older than she is. Her parents were both of above-average intelligence, and her family could be considered middle class. Although they were certainly not rich, they at least had the necessities, which is more than many families she knew had. Her childhood was fairly sheltered but she attended school and made a few friends there. She was an average student, getting grades of mostly Bs and Cs. Although these were similar to those of her friends, her parents were disappointed with her grades and let her know about that. They believed she should be doing better because they had done better in school and because her older brother did much better; he was an exceptional student.

Betty's main ambition, a typical one for girls at that time, was to get married and have a family. In the 1950s middle-class girls found a husband by attending college, which she did. Betty attended an all-girl college and majored in education, one of the acceptable majors for young women then. However, she dated infrequently probably because (1) she felt that the other women in her classes were wittier and more attractive (she often referred to herself as a Plain Jane, both in outward appearance and in personality) and (2) her father often forbade her to attend social functions held by the close-by, all-male academy, even though they were extremely well chaperoned. Despite these obstacles, Betty met and dated one man in college with whom she fell in love. Unfortunately, this young man did not return her feelings.

Betty earned her teaching degree and then taught for several years. While attending another college one summer to take additional education courses, she met a young man, Cole, who was also attending college. They dated, and after the summer, they continued a long-distance relationship by writing letters to each other. After six months, Cole proposed to her in a letter. She accepted. She was 26 at the time and he was 28. At that time, a woman who was 26 was considered "over the hill," with little chance of getting married. This was probably one reason she accepted his proposal. She saw it as her last opportunity for marriage. Betty's parents disapproved of the match but eventually came to accept it.

Betty gave up her teaching career, as was the practice at the time, to become a wife and eventually a mother. Unfortunately for Betty, married life was not what she expected. Cole was employed by a business that required him to do a great deal of traveling. Likewise, his job forced him, and his family, to move frequently. Eventually Betty became dissatisfied with moving every two to three years. She wanted roots and children and she thought that it was important that their children develop long-term friendships. After being married for five years, Betty and Cole had their first child, a son. Two years later Betty had a miscarriage and two years after that, a second son. Over time, Betty became more devoted to her children than to her husband. For example, her first child was allowed to be read four books and sing four songs before bedtime, but she granted her husband very little of her attention. The attention he did receive was often in the form of criticism.

After 15 years of marriage, Betty had had enough of moving around and the family bought a house in Connecticut. Her husband was able to obtain a position in his employer's New York City branch, and he commuted home on weekends. Cole's being a weekend husband and father certainly took its toll on Betty and Cole's marriage, but Betty continued to raise her two sons and attend her children's extracurricular activities. She also became an active member of her church, where she taught Sunday school and organized the church's social hour.

Now that her children are grown and have families of their own, Betty wonders why she should continue to live with a man she feels so distant from and how she could begin to feel needed again. She wishes she could relocate closer to one of her children, but they have families of their own, and she does not want to intrude.

APPLICATION QUESTIONS

Using Erikson's psychosocial stages of development (especially the fourth through the eighth), analyze Betty's life by answering the following questions.

1. Would Erikson's theory suggest that Betty's behavior is internally or externally motivated? What motivates it? Which system of personality is most involved in personality, according to the theory?

2. What is the crisis experienced in Erikson's fourth stage of psychosocial development? How did Betty resolve this stage? What was the outcome of the crisis? Was it favorable or unfavorable?

3. What is the crisis experienced in Erikson's fifth stage of psychosocial development? How did Betty resolve this stage? What was the outcome of the crisis? Was it favorable or unfavorable?

4. What is the crisis experienced in Erikson's sixth stage of psychosocial development? How did Betty resolve this stage? What was the outcome of the crisis? Was it favorable or unfavorable?

5. What is the crisis experienced in Erikson's seventh stage of psychosocial development? How did Betty resolve this stage? What was the outcome of the crisis? Was it favorable or unfavorable?

6. What could be expected in the eighth stage of Betty's life, according to Erikson's theory?

THEORY COMPARISON QUESTIONS

1. Which of Fromm's needs have been met for Betty? Which have not? Explain. How does Fromm's theory compare with Erikson's in their consideration of social influence?

2. How would Rogers' concept of conditions of worth explain Betty's career choice? Her marriage to Cole? How is the emphasis of Rogers' theory different from that of Erikson's?

3. At what Jungian stage could Betty be placed? Why? How do Jung's stages compare with those of Erikson?

Helpful Hints

Are you having a problem answering some of the application questions for Case 5 or 6? See if the following will help you.

You are probably familiar with the adolescence stage in Erikson's theory because his term, *identity crisis*, has found its way into our modern vocabulary and become mainstream. Interestingly, however, Erikson thought that much of our identity develops out of our career choice. This tends to occur a bit later today than in Erikson's time. Also, Erikson thought that women would have had a more difficult time in developing an identity because, at the time of his theory development, women typically did not pursue careers outside the home. Today this is not as much of an issue.

Some of the terms that Erikson used to describe stage crises and outcomes have a different meaning today than when Erikson was developing his theory.

For example, students are often confused about the idea of intimacy during the (early) young adulthood stage. Today we think of intimacy in sexual terms but Erikson used the term *intimacy* to describe emotionally close, caring relationships that could be either sexual or nonsexual in nature. *Generativity*, a term used in describing the crisis in the (middle) adulthood stage, is also a difficult term to understand because we do not use it readily today. Erikson used this term to describe concern for future generations. It is important to note that this concern refers to generations beyond our own family. Finally, the term *integrity* is often used today to describe honesty or morality. Erikson used this term to describe the crisis that occurs during the (old age) mature adulthood stage but in his theory it refers to an acceptance of, or satisfaction with, the way we have lived our lives.

Alfred Adler (1870–1937)

Individual Psychology
Why learn this theory?

Contributions

Alfred Adler's contributions to the field of personality are numerous. His writing on the relationship between birth order and personality development is often cited as one of his most important but, in general, his guide to parenting is very significant and more encompassing. Adler observed the importance of both the mother and the father in the development of a healthy personality in children and noted the significance of the early social environment. Specifically, Adler advised parents to neither neglect nor overindulge their children because this type of interaction would result in low social interest. A middle ground that balances the needs of the child with the needs of the parents is necessary. This cautionary warning is especially important today as parents become increasingly involved in their children's lives: home schooling them, driving them to multiple extracurricular activities, and intervening when their children make mistakes. It is not these activities per se that interfere with the emergence of a high level of social interest. Rather, it is a message that children receive when parents ignore their own needs completely in order to accommodate those of their children. When parents invest all their energy into their children's lives, and none into their own, the child never learns that other people have needs also, thereby resulting in low social interest, which Adler viewed as being the cause of maladjustment. Although most experts would disagree with that causal view, it is likely that a lack of social interest (i.e., a primary concern for oneself only) is a symptom of maladjustment, and certainly encouraging a concern for others, and discouraging self-centered behavior, are valuable goals.

Adler's belief in the value and uniqueness of the individual, including the fact that people have subjective perceptions, is likewise an important observation and a contribution to humanistic thought. Adler's other noteworthy contributions include his observation that human beings compensate for feelings of inferiority. He also observed, contrary to the suggestion of Freud, that although maladjusted people are unconsciously motivated, well-adjusted people were conscious of their behavior; they were aware of what they were doing and why. Additionally, his teleological view (i.e., that we are motivated by our perceptions of the future) is a notable contribution to the field and definitely a departure from Freud's causal view. Finally, Adler's style of life is a concept that has made its way into mainstream societal terminology: The general public widely uses the term "lifestyle" to reflect a concept similar to what Adler meant by "style of life."

Case Study 7
Alfred Adler

By almost anyone's standards, Martin is extremely successful. He is a criminal lawyer who earns approximately a half million dollars each year defending rich, and sometimes well-known, clients against criminal charges ranging from drunk driving and marijuana possession to murder. His salary allows him a life of luxury. He owns two houses, one in Connecticut that is worth a million dollars, from which he commutes to New York City to do most of his work, and a "cabin" in the mountains of Colorado where he vacations often and that is worth about a half million dollars. He owns a Jaguar, a Lexus, and a Range Rover. He buys designer clothes and eats at all the best restaurants. He attends the theater and art openings.

Martin's life has not always been luxurious, however. He actually came from very humble beginnings. He was born in a medium-sized city in a very Polish American neighborhood. His parents were working class, and neither parent finished high school. His mother stayed home with the children. Although his father was a carpenter by trade, he sometimes had trouble finding work because of discriminatory practices. Others did not want to hire him because they distrusted members of his ethnic group. At times, the family was eligible for welfare assistance, but his father refused to apply for it because it would have hurt his pride. Occasionally, the children went to bed hungry because of this.

Martin's mother was from a family that had more money than her husband's family did. She had gotten pregnant by Martin's father when she was just 19. Although her parents did not approve of the match, believing that she was marrying below her status, they forced Martin's mother into the marriage because of the pregnancy. Martin was the product of that pregnancy. After Martin's birth, it became very clear to his mother that she preferred the more affluent life she had lived when she was single, which eventually made her resent both Martin and his father. As staunch Catholics, however, they never considered divorce, and the couple had two more children.

Neither parent was very affectionate toward the children, and sometimes not even the children's basic physical needs were met, especially when Martin's father was out of work. Martin often felt alone and commented at one point that neither of his parents really loved him.

Martin felt embarrassed by his humble beginnings. In particular, he was embarrassed by his ethnic background, his parent's lack of education, and his lack of material goods. He became determined to rise above his early station in life and achieve a more successful and sophisticated life. Martin does not want to think about or discuss his childhood. On the very rare occasion when he does think about his past, he recalls a very early memory about another child who had been unjustly accused of stealing an item from a store. The item had actually fallen down and rolled under the counter. Martin defended the child and showed the store clerk the dropped item, thus saving an innocent child from being unjustly punished.

Martin was an excellent student in grade school and high school; he earned a full scholarship to the University of Michigan where he graduated with honors; he then attended Harvard Law School. He passed the bar the first time around. Other students and some of his professors commented on Martin's penetrating intellect and his unwavering determination to excel in academics. However, they also remarked about how few friendships he had, his lack of female companionship, and his disinterest in any of the other activities on campus that were either of entertainment value or contributed to the well-being of the university.

Martin started at a well-known law firm and was on the fast track toward a partnership, but he became disgruntled with the politics of the firm and the social games being played. He left to start a new firm of his own, and some of his clients went with him. His reputation as a defense lawyer grew quickly, and he soon found his firm and his wallet growing in size.

Because he is well known, several organizations have asked him to be on their boards of directors, but he has refused all of them. Martin is not active in any community activities and does no volunteer work, not even pro bono legal work.

APPLICATION QUESTIONS

Using Adler's theory of individual psychology, analyze Martin's life by answering the following questions.

1. What evidence is there that Martin had feelings of inferiority?
2. According to Adler's theory, how did feelings of inferiority influence Martin's behavior? What influence did these beliefs of inferiority have on his striving for superiority?

3. According to Adler's theory, what was Martin's goal? What was Martin's unique style of life that could be used to achieve this goal? Provide evidence for your answer.

4. Did Martin have a high or a low level of social interest? What does this imply about his personality and adjustment? What is the cause of this level of social interest?

5. What did Adler say about birth order that would apply to Martin's life?

THEORY COMPARISON QUESTIONS

1. How could Horney's concept of basic anxiety explain Martin's exaggerated independence? What mechanisms are used by Martin to help him deal with basic anxiety? How does Adler's concept of social interest compare with Horney's trend of moving away from people?

2. How do Adler's safeguarding tendencies compare with Horney's neurotic trends? Explain Martin's lack of relationships using these two concepts.

3. How does Adler's superiority complex compare with Horney's concept of idealized self?

4. According to Bowlby and Ainsworth, what type of attachment style does Martin display? Explain. What would be the source of this type of attachment style?

Case Study 8
Alfred Adler

Toshimi is a ballet dancer and teacher. She has her own ballet school in Detroit and teaches dozens of children, mostly girls, how to *plié,* the correct positions for their arms and legs, and how to go *en pointe.* Looking at her now, anyone would think that she is the epitome of health. She is thin, with an athletic build, strong yet graceful, and very coordinated. Her school is the best in the city, and a few of her students have gone on to train and dance with prestigious dance companies.

Toshimi was not always athletic or graceful, though. As a child, she was very sickly and, because of a variety of health problems, was not able to play physical games like tag and baseball very well with other children. She was born prematurely and almost died a few days later from a respiratory infection. Later in childhood, she developed a severe case of tuberculosis, from which she gradually recovered. As she was an only child, her parents became overprotective of Toshimi and for years encouraged her to "take it easy," to not run around very much, and to not become too excited. Essentially, they encouraged Toshimi to become fragile. Her inactivity left her awkward and out of shape, which, in turn, resulted in an ineptitude for childhood games. She felt as though her friends were better than she was, at least in terms of physical activity, and unfortunately she was right. In fact, one of her earliest memories was of not being chosen to be on anyone's baseball team. The other children chose other friends to be on the two teams but both team captains, although they liked Toshimi, refused to let her on their team because she was too clumsy and slow. Toshimi, feeling very embarrassed, returned home alone and turned on the television. As she flipped through the channels, a program on PBS caught her eye. She saw women and men in beautiful costumes performing incredible physical feats. The women were able to stand on their toes, and both the men and women were able to perform graceful leaps. As she

28

watched the *Swan Lake* ballet, Toshimi became determined. Rather than leading to depression, thinking about this painful experience of not being chosen for a team made Toshimi very determined to become healthy and physically fit. More than anything, she wanted to be good at some kind of physical activity and to have others respect her athleticism.

Toshimi nagged her overprotective parents into letting her take ballet lessons. They reluctantly gave in, thinking (incorrectly) that dance was not very strenuous. They loved their daughter and did not want to deny her anything. At first, Toshimi was incredibly incompetent and clumsy in dance class, but she had a patient and understanding teacher who discouraged the other children from snickering. Toshimi gradually became stronger and more coordinated. Eventually, she started to show some talent for the ballet, especially for choreography. Her teacher also noted her determination and talent and discussed the possibility of training for a career in dance. After a discussion with her parents, Toshimi was allowed to take extra dance classes at a summer camp for dancers, and she did so for a number of years. At first, the camp dance teacher was reluctant to take Toshimi as a student because she was older than most of the girls, but was convinced to work with Toshimi for a short time and then determine whether Toshimi should stay on. Soon, it was very clear that Toshimi had talent. She stood out in a performance, and she was a gifted choreographer.

Toshimi's life changed dramatically when she moved to live with the dancers at the camp. She found that her every whim was no longer satisfied and that she had to wait her turn for various things—from brushing her teeth, to getting food, to using the phone to call her parents, to talking and working with her teacher. Although she found it difficult, Toshimi eventually adjusted to this lifestyle and in the process found herself caring for some of the younger girls. She was the oldest and found herself in the role of a big sister. She comforted the younger girls and gave them advice when they asked for it. They looked up to her, especially when they needed comfort. This was quite a change for Toshimi. When she had lived with her parents, it was she who needed comforting, for example, as in the time when no one wanted her on their baseball team. Now her role was reversed.

Although Toshimi showed determination and talent, her delay in taking dance lessons put her at a disadvantage. Furthermore, because of discriminatory practices at that time, it was very difficult for a woman of Asian descent (or any other minority) to begin a career as a professional dancer. Although disappointed, Toshimi would not be stopped from pursuing her dream. She continued to take dance lessons, and in college she majored in dance and minored in business. When she completed her degree, she opened her own dance studio with a loan from her parents and began giving dance lessons to children. Her reputation as an experienced, talented, and patient ballet teacher grew, and her enrollment enlarged. Today there is a waiting list to begin lessons at her school. She is also beginning to get a reputation regionally and even nationally because a number of her students have been accepted to train with such prestigious ballet companies as the New York City Ballet and the American Ballet Theater.

APPLICATION QUESTIONS

Using Adler's theory of individual psychology, analyze Toshimi's life by answering the following questions.

1. What is the motivation behind Toshimi's career choice, according to Adler's theory?

2. According to Adler's theory, what was Toshimi's goal? What was Toshimi's unique style of life that could be used to achieve this goal? Provide evidence for your answer.

3. Does Toshimi have a high or low level of social interest? What does this imply about her personality and adjustment? What is the cause of this level of social interest?

4. What did Adler say about birth order that would apply to Toshimi's life?

THEORY COMPARISON QUESTIONS

1. What other theory, besides Adler's, could explain Toshimi's career choice? How?

2. How do Adler's thoughts on parenting compare with Erikson's? Would Adler consider Toshimi's parents as having good parenting skills? Would Erikson?

3. Use Rotter's concepts of expectancy and reinforcement value to explain Toshimi's nagging of her parents to take ballet despite their hesitance.

Helpful Hints

Are you having a problem answering some of the application questions for Case 7 or 8? See if the following will help you.

Remember that, according to Adler, all people strive for success or superiority because we are motivated to overcome innate feelings of inferiority experienced when we are babies. But how people define success or superiority varies from person to person.

Thus, each individual's goals are unique. Likewise, how each individual strives to reach that goal varies, even if two people seem to be striving for the same goal. The way a person strives to meet his or her goal (or strive for success) is referred to as *style of life*. The key to identifying style of life lies in one's earliest memory because that memory has psychological significance for the individual and has been repeatedly considered.

Karen Horney (1885–1952)

Psychoanalytic Social Theory
Why learn this theory?

Contributions

Although her theory is somewhat repetitive, the strength of Horney's theory is her clear description of the neurotic personality, including her neurotic trends and neurotic needs. While Horney's theory is not practical in the sense that she did not specify techniques that are best to manage the neurotic personality, just being able to label and understand these behaviors is helpful to therapists in identifying them. For non-therapists, being familiar with these concepts is also helpful as a coping mechanism: Being aware of Horney's secondary defenses, and her concept of the idealized self, the tendency for neurotics to see themselves in glorified ways, assists us in managing some of the more frustrating behaviors of neurotics with whom we interact at work, school, or in our family life.

Horney contributed to many other areas of personality psychology as well. For example, she was among the first to voice a feminist criticism of Freud's theory, and her writings emphasized the role of culture in the development of personality. But her observation and understanding of the neurotic personality really was her most significant contribution to the field. She showed us that when people feel unloved they engage in behaviors to compensate for it, either pushing people away so people won't hurt us, being submissive so that others will love us, or using others before they use us.

Case Study 9

Karen Horney

Samara just cannot understand why she is still single at age 35 when all her friends are happily married. She sees herself as loving, generous, and unselfish. Certainly she is sensitive to the needs of others, much more so than her friends seem to be. Her friends seem to criticize their husbands; she would never do that. Certainly, she would not force her mate into going to see a movie or play that she wanted to see but that he did not.

Getting married is especially important to Samara because she was raised in a very traditional Middle Eastern household where the role of the woman is to be someone's wife and mother. It isn't that she doesn't try to establish relationships. In fact, she has had many relationships with men; they just don't last. For example, her last boyfriend, Tom, broke up with her after six months. He claimed that she was too pushy and possessive. Samara was pushing him to get married, and he was not ready for that kind of commitment yet. He was also concerned about her jealousy. Samara hated it when Tom showed attention to other women—even though the attention was platonic. Tom has a number of women friends and keeps in touch with them by talking on the telephone. He also goes to lunch with them occasionally. Likewise, Tom has a number of female colleagues at work. Samara often complained to Tom that he spent too much time with other women and not enough time with her. Even though Tom continuously tried to reassure Samara that these relationships with women were nonsexual and that they were friends to him, not potential dates, Samara continued to discourage these relationships. Samara was terrified that Tom would find these other women more attractive than she and desert her. She just did not want to be alone again.

But Samara is rarely "alone." She goes from a breakup to another relationship very quickly. She had broken up with another boyfriend, Fred, two weeks before she met Tom and started dating him. One month before she started dating Fred, she experienced another breakup, this time initiated by Paul. The breakup with Paul was fairly vicious, and again, Samara had trouble understanding why it happened. She had done her best to make Paul happy. She let him decide where they would go and what they would do on dates. She even let him decide what to order for her at restaurants. When Paul would ask her what she wanted to do, she always replied, "Whatever you want." Samara just couldn't understand how men could not appreciate what a giving, unselfish person she was.

She was always there for her current boyfriend. When he was having a difficult time, she would listen to his problems very attentively and help him feel better. She would do this even when she too had a problem she wanted to discuss, but she always put his needs before her own. Instead of appreciating these qualities, the men she dated found them unappealing. At the time of their breakup, Paul, for example, complained that Samara was too mousy, that he did not know what she liked to do or even eat! He said that he could not get to know her and therefore did not want a relationship with her. He found her submissiveness annoying, not endearing. He also complained, like Tom, about Samara's possessiveness. Paul sometimes wanted to spend time alone or with his male friends, but Samara resented this time away from her. In fact, the week before they broke up, Samara and Paul had a huge argument about Paul's friends. Samara had gone shopping and was in the process of cooking an elaborate meal—Paul's favorite— but Paul called to tell her that he ran into an old buddy who was in town just for the night and that he couldn't see her that evening; he was going to go out with his buddy. Paul had no idea that she was planning to cook a big meal for him; he thought they would be going out for a burger at his favorite bar. Samara became angry because of her wasted effort and told him how unappreciative he was. He in turn complained about her unreasonable assumptions and possessiveness. That argument led to their breakup the following week.

Now, after the breakup with Tom, Samara is again asking friends to fix her up. As she commiserates with her friends, she tells them that all she wants is someone to love her, that if you have love, you have everything. She wonders if she will ever find the right man.

APPLICATION QUESTIONS

Using Horney's psychoanalytic social theory, analyze Samara's behavior by answering the following questions.

1. Which of Horney's neurotic trends (or basic adjustments) is Samara demonstrating? Explain.

2. Which of Horney's neurotic needs does Samara demonstrate? Find examples in the case study.

3. According to Horney's theory, what is the cause of Samara's neurotic behavior?

4. Is Samara's self-image an accurate one? How could Horney's theory explain the discrepancy between Samara's idealized versus real image of herself?

THEORY COMPARISON QUESTIONS

1. Is there a discrepancy between Samara's organismic self and her perceived or ideal self? Explain. How do Horney's concepts of idealized and real selves compare with Rogers' concepts of organismic, perceived, and ideal selves?

2. How can Kelly's individuality corollary explain the difference in opinion between Samara and her boyfriends on the status of their relationships?

3. Use Rotter's concept of locus of control to explain Samara's relationships with men.

Case Study 10
Karen Horney

At the age of 23, Shimin has just earned his master's degree in mathematics and is about to begin his first, full-time, permanent position at a General Motors Research Facility. He had other part-time jobs to get him through his education, but now he has finally begun his career. One of these part-time jobs was as an instructor in the department where he was completing his master's degree requirements. This position initially required that Shimin teach three sections of an introductory level math course each semester in return for a tuition waver and a small stipend.

Shimin did not enjoy his teaching experience, and, apparently, his students did not either. Shimin was displeased with his students' lack of enthusiasm. He complained that his students were not really trying to learn and that they were not interested in the material. He frequently found himself comparing what he had been as a freshman to the students whom he was now teaching, and he always found that his perception of himself at that time was more favorable than his view of his students. He was more interested, more enthusiastic, worked harder and longer, was more persistent, and so on. His students complained that Shimin was difficult to understand, that he covered the material too quickly, and that he was unapproachable. They complained that he made them feel stupid when they asked questions, and so they stopped asking questions. Moreover, their grades suffered because of it. These complaints made their way back to the mathematics department chair, and she discussed them with Shimin.

Shimin did not enjoy teaching anyway, so the chair and Shimin thought it would be best if he would not teach the following semester and become a teaching assistant for a professor instead. His duties would be grading exams and homework. This suited him much better, and Shimin was quite efficient at his task, earning the respect of his professor.

Shimin's academic performance was superior as well. He earned excellent grades in his graduate classes and he finished his master's thesis on time. In fact,

35

everyone, including his advisor, was quite surprised he had completed his thesis and was asking for an appropriate date for his defense. He had met with his advisor a minimal number of times, although he did send his advisor a memo once a month about his progress on his thesis. Most other students work closely with their thesis advisors and meet with them frequently. In recommendation letters that were sent out to prospective employers, Shimin's advisor noted how independent he was.

Not surprisingly, Shimin was a superior student before graduate school, in both high school and college. In high school, he was an "ideal" student. He completed his assignments diligently, aced his exams, and was never disruptive in class. In fact, he rarely spoke in class unless he was asked a direct question, and then he usually answered correctly. He gained a reputation for being self-motivated. His teachers and guidance counselors did not need to spend much time with him because he always worked things out on his own. He actually preferred things that way because he felt he could always depend on himself but that one could not always depend on someone else's help. One reason he could rely so much on himself to learn and to make decisions was because he was an avid reader and computer whiz. He could do research on something in the library or on the Internet and did not need to discuss it with anyone else or ask anyone questions.

This same pattern of behavior continued in college, with Shimin excelling academically, despite the fact that he was an international student in the United States from Hong Kong whose second language was English. One professor who did begin to get to know Shimin suggested that he needed to contribute more to class discussion. This was a disturbing concept to Shimin, who until then had used his academic success to discourage interaction with others. He thought that if one doesn't have any questions, one didn't need to talk in class. Shimin dismissed this idea of talking in class as being an idiosyncrasy of the professor. Certainly, independence and self-sufficiency were much better and would earn him the respect of others, or so he believed.

By his own choosing, Shimin has not had much of a social life. He rarely dates. Although he says that this is because he is too busy, it is actually because he hates the process of getting to know someone. He is reluctant to talk about himself and finds it difficult to answer questions about himself on first dates. He did not get to know many other students in college or graduate school because he did not live in the dorms. He preferred to rent an apartment so that he could live on his own. In both college and graduate school, Shimin joined various clubs and organizations, but again, he rarely made it to the meetings because he was "too busy."

APPLICATION QUESTIONS

Using Horney's psychoanalytic social theory, analyze Shimin's behavior by answering the following questions.

1. How does Shimin combat basic anxiety, according to Horney's theory?

2. Which of Horney's neurotic needs does Shimin display?

3. Which of Horney's secondary defenses is Shimin using when he says he is too busy to join clubs or go on dates? Explain.

THEORY COMPARISON QUESTIONS

1. Use another theory, besides Horney's, to explain Shimin's antisocial behavior.

2. How do Horney's and Fromm's emphasis on social influences on behavior compare?

3. How does Adler's concept of social interest compare with Horney's concept of withdrawing from others? Use both of these concepts to explain Shimin's avoidance of close relationships.

Helpful Hints

Are you having a problem answering some of the application questions for Case 9 or 10? See if the following will help you.

Horney's theory is a bit redundant. She discusses four basic ways that people protect themselves against basic anxiety (affection; submissiveness; striving for power, prestige, or possessions; and withdrawal), ten neurotic needs, and three neurotic trends (moving toward people, moving against people, and moving away from people). In actuality these concepts all overlap.

For example, the trend of moving toward people (the compliant personality) would include the neurotic needs for affection and approval, for a partner, and to restrict one's life within narrow borders. One can also see that this would include two ways that people protect themselves against basic anxiety: affection and submissiveness. The neurotic trend of moving against people (the aggressive personality) would include the needs for power, to exploit others, for prestige or social recognition, for personal admiration, and for ambition and personal achievement. This would include using striving for power, prestige, or possessions to protect oneself against basic anxiety. Finally, the neurotic trend of moving away from people (the detached personality) would include the needs for self-sufficiency and independence and for perfection and unassailability. This reflects the use of withdrawal to protect against basic anxiety.

Erich Fromm (1900–1980)

Humanistic Psychoanalysis
Why learn this theory?

Contributions

Although he had extensive training in psychoanalysis, Erich Fromm is best known for his influence on humanistic thought. His theory is referred to as humanistic psychoanalysis and his discussion of positive freedom (or self-realization) is especially noteworthy. Fromm's writing on this topic discouraged conformity and routine living and encouraged living creatively and meaningfully. He helped us to understand that we have the freedom to realize our potential but that many do not because freedom has both positive and negative characteristics. While freedom is liberating and growth-enriching, it also carries responsibility with it, and this responsibility frightens some people, preventing them from capitalizing on its growth-enriching prospects.

Fromm's writings on genuine love relationships are also significant, noting their growth-enriching possibilities. He made a distinction between genuine healthy love relationships and unhealthy pseudo-love relationships. He even attempted to define what a genuine love relationship is, suggesting that it consists of caring for another, a sense of responsibility toward that person, respect for them, and knowledge of them. He noted that healthy people are able to retain their individuality and uniqueness in love relationships. A person who displays the productive (healthy) character orientation combines this genuine love experience with creative living and meaningful work. For Fromm, these are the characteristics that define a well-adjusted person.

Other contributions of Fromm include his discussion of human needs, which were precursors to the more recently developed needs discussed by Maslow and Rogers. Fromm's concept of the human dilemma also bears mentioning: In his discussions about the human dilemma, Fromm observed that some people think too much. They overanalyze experiences so that it is difficult to enjoy them and, ultimately, makes it difficult for these people to function in everyday life. In sum, Fromm's theory influenced humanistic thought, but it also helped psychologists to understand adjustment, as well as maladjustment.

Case Study 11
Erich Fromm

It is Christmas Eve, and Jeff is basking in the glow of the Christmas tree and the fire in the fireplace. As he looks around the living room of his parents' house, he can clearly see the love in his family, and he smiles to himself. His parents are on the floor playing with their grandchildren, his children, and as he and his wife enter the living room with Christmas cookies and cocoa, the children rush for the snacks, squealing with excitement. It is like this every winter holiday season. Jeff and his wife, Ann, travel six hours by car with their children to spend a week with Jeff's parents, and this amounts to a daunting task. Jeff and Ann have to pack clothes not only for themselves but also for their children. When the children were younger, this also meant packing the everyday needs of babies and toddlers—bottles, nipples, diapers, bibs, and so forth, along with snacks, toys, and books to help keep the children amused during the long ride to Grandma and Grandpa's. Finally, there were all the Christmas presents. This seemed to be the hardest task, especially when the children were younger and believed in Santa Claus. It was difficult to hide the presents in such a packed and cramped car and to shuffle them inside his parents' house before Christmas to set them up for Christmas morning. There was also the occasional lake-effect snow that sometimes hit at this time of year and that could make driving treacherous.

Still, neither he nor his wife would miss this event for anything. During the holiday season, they would be able to visit with many relatives they were able to see only this one time each year. On Christmas Day and New Year's Day, his parents, Jeff's family, and his brother's and sister's families would get together, feast, and talk. All the children—the cousins—would get to know each other again and play together with their new toys.

Returning to his hometown was meaningful to Jeff and to his wife. For Jeff returning to his hometown helped him reconnect to the person he had been when he was growing up. Although Ann was not from Jeff's hometown of Batavia, she had no real family and was accepted readily into Jeff's family when they became engaged years ago. Returning to Batavia each winter was enjoyable for Ann as well as Jeff, because they saw so little of their family during the year and because, even though they had some close friends in Cleveland, where they lived, they had no family living in the area. Sometimes they felt lonely, especially when they heard of their friends being helped by their families who were located close by. This was especially true when their children were very small and babysitters did not show up when they were supposed to. Ann and Jeff often had to scramble for a sitter so they could both go to work. They also would have liked to spend a little more time alone as a couple and wished some family members were around to watch the kids and give them this opportunity. Beyond their wish for trustworthy babysitters, Jeff and Ann would have liked to share some of the everyday events of life with family. They wished Jeff's parents could see their grandchildren in school plays and little league. For Ann and Jeff, family has always been important, and they wanted to instill this value in their children. Jeff remembers the holiday seasons when he was growing up and how his family always had Thanksgiving dinner with his cousins' family and how Christmas and New Year's were also shared with others. He wanted his children to have these kinds of enjoyable memories when they grew up. Likewise, Jeff and Ann wanted their children to understand where they came from and to be aware of their cultural heritage.

The loneliness of living away from family caused Jeff and Ann to consider moving back to the small town outside of Rochester where Jeff grew up, especially when they first moved to Cleveland. This was not a realistic consideration, however; it was more of a wish. There were no job opportunities in Batavia in Jeff's type of work, and Ann was settled in her career as well. Although exciting, the move to Cleveland had also been frightening for both Ann and Jeff. They initially thought that the move would be good for them and their new marriage, because there would be no family influences. But it was also stressful and scary to be completely on their own. They had no one to ask advice from about houses they considered buying or other such decisions.

Jeff and Ann did well on their own, with minimal hassles. Both found their work rewarding and were optimistic about continuing their careers. Jeff worked for a manufacturing company that also cared about the environment and recycled extensively. He felt good about the company's efforts to improve the environment and that the company encouraged its workers to come up with ideas that would benefit both the company and the environment. Ann was a computer programmer and enjoyed the daily challenges of creating new programs that made other people's work easier. Both Ann and Jeff were aware that they had unique talents that benefited their employers, and they felt confident in their positions, despite the popular trend of downsizing.

Likewise, Jeff and Ann's marriage was strong. No family is perfect and theirs was no exception; there were the usual squabbles about children and arguments revolving around money and housekeeping. Nevertheless, Jeff and Ann truly cared about each other and about their children, and their children similarly loved their parents and their siblings. Jeff and Ann had similar views about how to live their lives to make them meaningful and tried to instill their value system in their children. In particular, Jeff and Ann wanted their children to believe that it was important to somehow make the world a better place than the way they found it. Both Jeff and Ann believed that their work did this, and they hoped that their children would eventually find work that was meaningful as well.

APPLICATION QUESTIONS

Using Fromm's humanistic psychoanalytic theory, analyze Jeff and Ann's behavior by answering the following questions.

1. How could Fromm's theory explain Jeff and Ann's return to Batavia every holiday season, despite the hardships?
2. Why do people, in general, and Jeff and Ann, in particular, marry or form other close relationships, according to Fromm's theory?
3. What is the transcendence need, according to Fromm? Has it been fulfilled by Ann and Jeff? Explain.
4. What is the identity need, according to Fromm? Has it been fulfilled by Ann and Jeff? Explain.
5. What is the excitation and stimulation need, according to Fromm? Has it been fulfilled by Ann and Jeff? Explain.
6. What is Jeff and Ann's frame of orientation, according to Fromm's theory?
7. What character orientation, according to Fromm, would Ann and Jeff belong to?
8. How could Fromm's theory explain Jeff and Ann's mixed feelings about initially moving to Cleveland?

THEORY COMPARISON QUESTIONS

1. How do Fromm's needs compare with Rogers' needs? With Maslow's?
2. How could behaviorism explain Jeff and Ann's return to Batavia every holiday season? How does the behavioral motivation emphasized by behaviorism compare with that of Fromm's theory?
3. How could evolutionary psychology explain Ann and Jeff getting married and having children? How does this explanation compare with that of Fromm?

Case Study 12
Erich Fromm

Andrea is about to embark on an obligatory visit to her remaining family for a week. She visits once a year, and every year she dreads it. Each visit is stressful, and, once she arrives at her mother's house, she feels like an outsider. It seems as though Andrea was always the outsider, even as a child. Her sister Marla was the favored daughter and seemed to encourage the favoritism by doing whatever their mother wanted instead of fulfilling her own needs and developing her own personality. Andrea, on the other hand, often irritated her mother because as a child she insisted on doing things her way. Even as an adult, Andrea continued to behave in certain ways of which their mother disapproved. It wasn't that Andrea wanted to have harmful or damaging experiences; she just wanted to do all the things that other children and, later, young adults always wanted to do. She wanted to go out with friends, have a few drinks, dance, and so on, but her mother disapproved of this behavior. It wasn't that her mother said anything. It was more an unspoken message conveyed by a disapproving look or tone of voice. Marla, on the other hand, did not want to risk this subtle form of disapproval and so she rarely went out. Over time, Andrea's mother seemed to have gained more control over Marla's behavior, and their relationship had deepened into an unhealthy dependence.

Today, when Andrea visits, she feels left out, as though Marla and her mother have formed a clique that Andrea is not part of. When Marla and her mother talk, they look directly at each other, as though they are talking only to each other, even though Andrea is in the room. They even consult each other about whether they should have a snack and sometimes share cups of coffee. Although Marla has her own home, she and her mother see each other every day after work and have dinner together, sometimes at her mother's house, sometimes at Marla's. They have keys to each other's houses and let themselves in whenever it suits them. All these activities exclude Andrea and make her feel uncomfortable.

It pains Andrea to see how dependent Marla is on their mother, and she wishes her sister had a different kind of life. Yet, nothing Andrea does seems to lessen the bond between Marla and her mother. When Andrea still lived at home, she would ask Marla to go out with her and her friends, but most times Marla declined to go. When Andrea moved away from her hometown, she would invite Marla down for a visit, but invariably Marla assumed that their mother was invited too and they would visit together.

This inability to travel without her mother began years ago. When Andrea graduated from college, she wanted to treat herself to a vacation and had arranged for her and Marla to go to Maine. Then, as they were discussing the vacation over coffee at their mother's house, their mother mentioned that she wished she could go. Marla, without consulting Andrea, asked their mother to join them. Their mother immediately jumped at the chance, and the three of them traveled together. This was very disappointing for Andrea, who was looking forward to going on her first vacation without a parent. From her perspective, the vacation was a disaster.

After they went out for drinks the first night of vacation with some of the fellow travelers of their age, Marla and Andrea were met with disapproving looks when they walked into the room they shared with their mother. Their mother was sitting in a chair, frowning, and expressed how worried she was about them. That was the last outing they had with the other young people. For the rest of the trip, Marla and their mother paired off and seemed to exclude Andrea; she felt like a third wheel, even though she was the one who initiated the vacation. Even today, at the age of 35, Marla still goes on vacation only with her mother. Likewise, she often invites her mother to go out with her and the few friends she sees occasionally. Andrea has given up trying to do things alone with Marla. Discussing the relationship between Marla and her mother is out of the question because Marla rebuffs any attempt at this type of conversation.

Other things also bother Andrea about her family visits. For example, she is often bored. Neither her mother nor her sister is very busy. Their main activities are working at their jobs and spending time with each other. Andrea, on the other hand, enjoys going shopping and going to restaurants, museums, and other cultural activities. She frequently goes out on weekends, whereas her family rarely does. This lack of activity places a lot of pressure on Andrea. Because she visits only once a year, her mother and her sister assume that she will spend all her time with them. But she would like to see a few friends that she grew up with on her visit as well. Unfortunately, just as when she was younger, she faces disapproval when she tries to see other people besides her sister and her mother. She wishes her family would be more active and her sister would be more independent.

APPLICATION QUESTIONS

Using Fromm's humanistic psychoanalytic theory, analyze Marla's behavior by answering the following questions.

1. What type of mother fixation could describe the relationship between Marla and her mother, according to Fromm? According to the theory, why is this behavior displayed?

2. What character orientation, according to Fromm's theory, would best describe Marla?

3. Which of Fromm's existential needs are met for Marla? Which are not? Explain.

4. Which mechanism of escape from freedom has Marla adopted? Explain.

THEORY COMPARISON QUESTIONS

1. What other theories, besides Fromm's, could explain Marla's relationship with her mother? How?

2. Compare Horney's concept of submissiveness to combat basic anxiety with Fromm's concept of submitting to another to fulfill the relatedness need. Apply both of these concepts to Marla's relationship with her mother.

3. How does an excessively dependent personality (or character) develop, according to Freudian theory? How could these concepts explain Marla's relationship with her mother? How do Fromm's character orientations compare with Freud's? How do these concepts compare with traits in trait theories?

Helpful Hints

Are you having a problem answering some of the application questions for Case 11 or 12? See if the following will help you.

The gist of Fromm's theory is that as we have evolved and become more complex, we have become distanced from nature, which makes us uncomfortable or anxious. We use a variety of mechanisms to reduce these uncomfortable feelings. Some of these mechanisms are healthy; others are not. For example, Fromm suggested that basic anxiety developed out of feelings of being alone in the world. We use a variety of *mechanisms of escape* in order to reduce these feelings of loneliness and isolation. These include authoritarianism, the tendency to unite with a powerful partner; destructiveness, a desire to eliminate that which is threatening including people, objects, or institutions; and (automaton) conformity, unconditional acceptance

of, and obedience to, authority. Relatedly, Fromm discussed a number of personality disorders including incestuous symbiosis, an exaggerated dependence on a mother or mother figure whereby another person is almost inseparable from the mother figure. It is an extreme form of mother fixation, which is more common and not as harmful. Although this type of disorder and the aforementioned mechanisms of escape *appear* to reduce feelings of isolation, they are unhealthy ways of coping with anxiety. Fromm believed that we could live healthy lives through positive freedom (or self-realization), which was comprised of love and work. Through *genuine* love, and work, we could truly unite with others and reduce our feelings of isolation. Hence, out of the character orientations that Fromm discussed, only one, the productive character orientation, is viewed as healthy.

Harry Stack Sullivan
(1892–1949)

Interpersonal Personality Theory
Why learn this theory?

Contributions

Sullivan's interpersonal personality theory is not a popular theory in the United States and often is not included in personality theories courses. However, while many of his concepts and his writings are considered confusing and sometimes disorganized, Sullivan developed unique ideas that are central to understanding human behavior and adjustment. Sullivan is known for moving away from the Freudian assumption that "anatomy is destiny." Instead, Sullivan's view was that society, not biology, was important in the formation of personality. In fact, he was one of the first theorists to discuss the importance of a "chum," a best friend, in the development of interpersonal skills that later can lead to healthy personal relationships. Similarly, decades later, Carl Rogers suggested that talking to a good friend, one that is empathic and nonjudgmental, can be just as effective in promoting growth, as talking to a therapist. Thus, one of Sullivan's important contributions to the field of personality was his de-emphasis of sexual motivation as a factor contributing to behavior and his emphasis on the importance of interpersonal relationships.

Sullivan's emphasis on the influence of interpersonal relationships is also exemplified in his concept of the need for tenderness, a unique need that few, if any, other theorists describe. Similar to concepts discussed by object relations theorists, this concept laid the foundation for the development of attachment theory. It described interactions between child and caregiver that are necessary in order to raise a psychologically healthy child. His theory, therefore, can be seen as a guide that promotes good parenting skills.

Case Study 13
Harry Stack Sullivan

Stacy, Caucasian and 26 years old, is a waitress. She is very good at what she does, primarily because she is so consumed with making sure all her customers' needs are met, even when they seem unreasonable. Her boss likes that about her because she keeps the customers happy. An example that illustrates her skill involves a customer who had placed an order for country-fried steak. When she brought it to him, he was dissatisfied with just about everything about it: He asked for more gravy on both his meat and mashed potatoes; he demanded a larger portion of vegetables, extra rolls, and said that the entire order needed to be heated up more. Stacy apologized profusely and brought back an order that was much more to his liking, without batting an eye. Most of the other waitresses she worked with would have brought this customer's order back but would have found other ways to get back at him. They certainly would not have apologized to him because there really was nothing wrong with the order.

Stacy was used to trying to please others. She had been doing it her entire life. As a child, throughout adolescence, and now throughout young adulthood, Stacy had always been submissive, sometimes to the point that others found her annoying.

As the third of four children raised by a single mother, Stacy craved her mom's attention but rarely received it. Her two older brothers were quite rambunctious and seemed to be always getting into some kind of trouble that their mother had to help get them out of. Her younger sister was born only 13 months after Stacy, 6 months after their father had left them. Although their mother loved them all, she found it difficult to give all her children the attention they needed and wanted. This was especially true of Stacy, who experienced the prototypical middle-child syndrome: her older siblings demanded their mother's attention and were used to getting it, and her younger sister needed their mother's attention because she was a baby. This did not leave much time for Stacy.

When Stacy did get her mother's attention as a preschool-age child, it was often precisely because she was not demanding it. Her mother would often make comments to Stacy such as, "Thank goodness you aren't asking me to do something too!" Although this does not sound endearing, Stacy's mother always said it with a sense of humor, and it did not hurt Stacy's feelings, but rather, it made her feel good. Like most children, Stacy also wanted to please her mother and would often do things like try to help her mom clean the kitchen or help with her baby sister. When Stacy did this, her mother would give her a rare hug and thank her. What Stacy learned from these experiences was that to gain someone else's attention or love, one needed to not make demands and, instead, do things for that person.

This submissive pattern of behavior continued into the realms of school and friendships. Stacy was an average student in early grade school. She was quiet in school and rarely volunteered answers in class or demanded the teacher's time. She also had some difficulty in establishing friendships with the other children. She was hesitant in approaching them and asking them to play with her. As a way to fit in with the other children, she would always play whatever they wanted and how they wanted, regardless of whether she wanted to or not. Not surprisingly, the other children tolerated Stacy but often took advantage of her, giving her the roles to play in their games that were most undesirable, such as the bad guys, while the other children played the roles of good guys like cops or superheroes. Other children had best friends, but Stacy did not.

In later grade school years, she also had trouble forming friendships with the other girls. It wasn't that they genuinely disliked her. She just never initiated any contact with them. The other girls called each other and invited each other over to their houses, but Stacy never took these initiatives.

In junior high, Stacy became interested in boys, just like the other girls did. Like the other girls, she read magazines that included stories about relationships between girls and boys. These stories had a similar theme: the girl often required a boy's help to solve a problem. When he solved the problem, he became interested in the girl. Or, by the girls changing in such a way that pleased the boys, the girls were able to establish relationships with them. Once again, Stacy learned that doing what others wanted is what gets them to like you and to become your friend or boyfriend.

Stacy became increasingly attractive during adolescence. This physical attractiveness, along with the boys thinking that Stacy was very agreeable, allowed Stacy to begin romantic relationships. Because of Stacy's inability to assert herself, she began to have sex shortly after she started dating. When her boyfriends asked her for sex, she often agreed because she was afraid they would leave her if she did not. Unfortunately, they often broke off the relationship anyway. Shortly after a breakup, another boy would ask Stacy out. She was getting a reputation for being promiscuous.

These types of relationships continued in high school and, in one case, resulted in unfortunate consequences. Stacy met a young man while she was in high school, and initially she was pleased with their relationship. The one thing she did not like or understand was his temper. He would often lose his temper and blame Stacy for whatever it was that set him off. Initially, his outbursts involved only yelling but eventually it escalated into pushing and shoving and finally other more serious forms of physical abuse. While Stacy was in this relationship, she continuously tried to please her boyfriend and wondered what it was that she was doing wrong. Stacy's mother forbade her to continue the relationship after she saw bruises on Stacy's body.

Now as an adult, Stacy is still searching for an intimate relationship. She still does not have any female friends, partly because she does not initiate friendships and partly because the other women she works with do not initiate them either. Although they don't mind working with Stacy, they view her as a kind of wimp. Likewise, although she dates, her relationships with men do not last long because the men feel they cannot get to know Stacy if she is continually trying to do only things that they like to do and talk about things that they want to talk about. They feel as though the relationship is very one-sided and this makes them uncomfortable.

APPLICATION QUESTIONS

Using Sullivan's interpersonal personality theory, analyze Stacy's behavior by answering the following questions.

1. How could Stacy's interactions be characterized? How could these interactions be considered "personality," according to Sullivan's theory?

2. What did Stacy experience during Sullivan's juvenile era? How did these experiences affect her personality?

3. What did Stacy experience during Sullivan's preadolescence stage? How did these experiences affect her personality?

4. What did Stacy experience during Sullivan's early adolescence stage? How did these experiences affect her personality?

5. What did Stacy experience during Sullivan's late adolescence stage? How did these experiences affect her personality?

6. What did Stacy experience during Sullivan's adulthood stage? How did these experiences affect her personality?

7. What would Stacy have to do to form a true relationship, according to Sullivan's theory?

8. Which of Sullivan's needs were fulfilled for Stacy? Provide evidence for your answer.

THEORY COMPARISON QUESTIONS

1. Which other theories, besides Sullivan's, could also explain Stacy's behavior? How?

2. How could evolutionary psychology explain Stacy's relationships with men? How does this compare with Sullivan's explanation?

3. According to Maslow, which of Stacy's needs have been fulfilled? How do Maslow's needs compare with Sullivan's?

Case Study 14
Harry Stack Sullivan

As Brian approaches his sixth birthday, his mother Tammy reflects on the changes she has seen in him over the years. Brian was a demanding baby. As a first-time mother, Tammy wanted to do everything right and had tried to nurse Brian. Unfortunately, Tammy was not prepared for how long it took to breastfeed and the discomfort that is initially involved. It seemed like she started out with cracked nipples. While still in the hospital, Brian often latched onto Tammy's breast incorrectly, which resulted in her having bruised and cracked nipples that took time to heal. Sometimes Brian would refuse to nurse because he preferred the ease of sucking from a bottle; nurses had introduced the bottle to him in the hospital nursery. Even though Tammy eventually began to learn how to position Brian and how to get him to latch on correctly, nursing just wasn't comfortable for her. She hated having leaking breasts; even nursing pads didn't always help. She was exhausted from a difficult delivery and from the physical demands of producing enough milk to keep Brian satisfied. And he seemed to need a lot of milk. Brian nursed every couple of hours for 40 minutes each time, even at night. Because Tammy was the sole nighttime feeder, she got only an hour of sleep at a time. In fact, the first night home from the hospital, Brian was up just about all night. That, coupled with having been in labor for 19 hours and the hospital staff waking Tammy every couple of hours to take her temperature and blood pressure, made Tammy mentally and emotionally exhausted a couple of days after Brian was born. She began to feel resentful toward her husband who was getting more sleep than she and who was not in such physical pain; she began to wonder whether nursing was worth the effort. The lack of sleep and the discomfort of nursing combined to form a fairly unpleasant experience as she fed her child. After just two months, Tammy gave up nursing and bottle-fed Brian, who had no trouble adjusting to bottles. When she started bottle-feeding, Tammy was amazed at how much better she felt, how much more energy she had, and how enjoyable feeding Brian was. She was able to relax when she fed him and gazed at his round little face, often smiling to herself and to Brian.

Brian was a difficult baby in other ways as well. He did not sleep through the night regularly until he was past two years old. Much of his waking was probably caused by teething pain. Tammy and her husband, Phil, often joked about Brian's "witching hour": the time every evening when Brian would begin to cry uncontrollably and nothing they would do could calm him down. And, he could scream loudly. They tried holding him, singing to him, and walking him—nothing worked. He did not stop crying until he fell asleep for the night. Looking back on that experience, Tammy wonders if Brian had actually been hungry but, at the time, neither parent thought that was possible because he had eaten so recently before the onset of the crying fit.

As he grew older, Brian became increasingly cooperative. When he was three and a half or four, and talking adequately, Tammy was able to talk to Brian about his temper tantrums and various other unacceptable behaviors. Sometimes Brian would refer to himself as the "bad Brian" or the "good Brian." On the days he was in an agreeable mood, he would tell his mother that the "good Brian is here today." Now that he is approaching the age of six, however, he no longer refers to himself as two people.

Brian is turning out to be quite different than what he was as a baby. He is a confident, personable, intelligent little boy with a wonderful sense of humor. He also has quite an imagination. The latest item he has conjured up is "ghost monsters" who drink juice when no one is looking. When Tammy asks him "who did something" in the house, Brian's standard reply is "A ghost monster." This started when Brian was about four. He would forget that he drank all his juice, and when he went back for more, he would wonder where it had gone. He started blaming ghost monsters. Eventually, the ghost monsters took on their own characteristics. One had black, bushy hair and red eyes. Some were friendly; others were not. Not too long ago, Tammy heard Brian talking to his little sister about how they should have a tea party with the friendly ghost monsters. The last six years have certainly been eventful, but Tammy would not change any of it.

APPLICATION QUESTIONS

Using Sullivan's interpersonal personality theory, analyze Tammy's and Brian's behavior by answering the following questions.

1. What is a personification, according to Sullivan? Find examples of the good mother, bad mother, good me, and bad me in the case study.
2. Using Sullivan's theory, interpret Tammy and Brian's feeding experiences.

3. How could Sullivan's theory interpret Brian's "witching hour" and his subsequent falling asleep?

4. In which of Sullivan's stages would you place Brian at the end of the case? Explain.

5. What level of cognition does Brian display at the end of the case, according to Sullivan's theory? Explain. When did he begin to display this level?

THEORY COMPARISON QUESTIONS

1. How does Klein's discussion of the mother's breast as both good and bad compare with Sullivan's good mother/bad mother personification?

2. Use Bandura's concept of reciprocal determinism to explain Tammy and Brian's breastfeeding experiences. How does this compare with Sullivan's explanation?

3. Use Skinner's radical behaviorism to explain Tammy and Brian's breastfeeding experiences. How does this compare with Sullivan's explanation?

4. How does Sullivan's concept of the Need for Tenderness compare to Bowlby and Ainsworth's concept of attachment style?

Helpful Hints

Are you having a problem answering some of the application questions for Case 13 or 14? See if the following will help you.

Personality for Sullivan was interpersonal style. He believed that our personality developed only through interactions with others, starting with interactions (especially feeding experiences) with our mothers. Good feeding experiences resulted in the good nipple and good mother personification; bad feeding experiences resulted in the bad nipple and bad mother personification. These personifications (images) are vague and not necessarily accurate or applicable to the mother in particular; they may apply to a *mothering one*, someone who takes on the caretaker role. These

personifications fuse later in the childhood stage and the child's perception of the mother becomes more accurate. Even though Sullivan stressed the importance of interpersonal relationships and clear communication in his theory, many of the terms he used are more difficult to understand than is necessary. A *tension*, for example, is defined as a potential for action; an energy transformation simply refers to behavior; a *dynamism* is an enduring energy unit or fairly consistent way of behaving. And Sullivan's term *somnolent detachment* is a fancy way of saying that a baby cried him/herself to sleep. As you can see, the aforementioned terms such as personification, mothering one, and good/bad mother are also awkward to use.

John Bowlby (1907–1990) and Mary Ainsworth (1919–1999)

Attachment Theory
Why learn this theory?

Contributions

The work of John Bowlby and Mary Ainsworth is of value, not just in the field of personality psychology, but also in developmental psychology and clinical psychology. Their work demonstrated the influence of the parent–child relationship on adult adjustment, personality, and adult relationships. From a developmental perspective, Bowlby and Ainsworth's work is important in the understanding of emotional and social development in children. From a clinical perspective it is important in the understanding of attachment disorders and is useful in therapy with children.

Bowlby was dissatisfied with what he viewed as the unscientific approach of object relations theorists. This, combined with his interest in evolutionary psychology, led to a more scientific approach to understanding childhood emotional attachment. In fact, he viewed attachment as of evolutionary benefit: It helps the child to survive because it assists the child in

protection from potential predators and in securing resources to fulfill his/her physiological needs, that is, food, water, shelter, and so on. Because the child survives, the parent's genes are passed on and also survive. Ainsworth was especially important in developing a more scientific approach to understanding these concepts and relationships by conducting further research on them and refining them. She also developed an empirical method to measure attachment style in young children called the strange situation procedure.

This work has had a tremendous impact on the understanding of effective parenting styles. Because of it, we now understand the importance of a responsive, emotionally warm caregiver in the development of a well-adjusted child and, later, a well-adjusted adult. We also understand the importance of this type of environment in the later development of healthy, secure relationships.

Case Study 15

John Bowlby and
Mary Ainsworth

Tina wonders about two twins, aged 22 months, at the daycare center where she works. They are fraternal twins: one boy, David, and one girl, Chelsea. They are so different, she wonders how they could possibly be twins, despite the fact that they are both the same age. David and Chelsea started daycare when they were two but Tina noticed how different the twins were the first day they were dropped off. David was a little apprehensive about the new situation but Chelsea was inconsolable. David hugged and kissed his mother goodbye and was sad when he watched her leave but was easily distracted by the daycare staff. He quickly became curious about the toys he could play with and became engaged in a variety of activities. His sister, on the other hand, had a much more difficult time separating from her mother. When Chelsea's mother was in the process of leaving the daycare center that first day, Chelsea clung to her mother and wailed as though she were in pain. Her mother responded, not with sympathy or reassurance like she did with David. Rather, she seemed embarrassed and irritated by the display. She could be described as harsh with Chelsea, telling her to "Stop it! You are embarrassing me!" Tina noticed this that first day for two reasons: (1) because the mother interacted very differently with David than with Chelsea; and (2) because most parents feel bad about leaving their child in daycare, especially on the first day, and are typically sympathetic to their apprehension. But the twins' mother acted coldly to Chelsea. Chelsea's agitation continued throughout the day.

When the twins' mother came to pick them up later that first day, David was ecstatic to see his mother again. As soon as he spied her, he ran up to her, hugged her, and started to tell her about all the things he did. His mother was very responsive, smiling at him and hugging him back, asking him questions. But when Chelsea first saw that her mother had returned, her reaction was very different. She ran over to her mother and hugged her, but instead of seeming to be happy to see her, she immediately began to cry, saying that she missed her mother so much. Her mother was puzzled and again reacted differently to Chelsea than to David. The mother told Chelsea that she was "here now" and hugged Chelsea in a stiff, unconvincing manner. Tina wasn't entirely sure that the mother was glad to see Chelsea. Tina was further confused when she overheard the mother snap at Chelsea to "Stop crying!"

Chelsea's inability to be consoled when her mother left daycare continued for weeks after starting at the center. On one day, her mother dropped her off when the children were in the outdoor playground. As the mother was leaving, Chelsea grabbed onto the fence surrounding the playground, crying loudly for her mother to come back. As her mother continued to walk away, she crumpled to the ground and continued to cry even though Tina tried to comfort her and distract her.

Tina continued to notice differences in David and Chelsea's behavior and also in how the mother interacted differently with each twin throughout the months the twins attended the daycare center. Last week, the children went on a field trip to the zoo, and Chelsea and David's mother chaperoned. Although all the children from the daycare center enjoyed it, during the visit David was startled by the lion's roar, which was very loud. He ran to his mother, who stooped down to catch him, and buried his face into her shoulder. She was able to calm him down, telling him, "It's all right. The lion is just saying '"Hi!"' David responded quickly and waved to the lion replying "Hi" back. Interestingly, Chelsea also became frightened at one point during the field trip. A stranger approached her because she was so cute and told her that the dress she was wearing was very pretty and "did her mommy pick it out for her?" Much to the stranger's chagrin, Chelsea ran away from her, crying. Her mother really didn't try to console her but did pick her up. Instead, she told Chelsea that she was being silly and "to act like a big girl." Confusingly, Chelsea seemed to want to be held by her mother but when she was picked up she squirmed to be put back down and then held up her hands to be picked up again, which further irritated her mother.

Tina wonders if these different reactions in the twins are due to biological differences or something else. Are they due to the fact that one twin is a boy and the other is a girl? Is David more stable because he is male? Is Chelsea more emotional because she is female? Do the twins have different genetic makeups that caused these differences in temperament? Or are they due to the different way that their mother treats them?

APPLICATION QUESTIONS

Using Bowlby and Ainsworth's attachment theory, explain David and Chelsea's behavior by answering the following questions.

1. According to Bowlby and Ainsworth, what type of attachment style does David display? Chelsea? Explain.

2. According to Bowlby and Ainsworth, why are David and Chelsea's attachment styles different?

3. Describe Ainsworth's strange situation. What does it measure? If a researcher were to study David and Chelsea's reactions in Ainsworth's stranger situation, what type of observations would s/he be likely to make?

4. What are the three stages of separation anxiety, according to Bowlby? In which stage is Chelsea when she cannot be comforted by the daycare staff after her mother leaves her?

5. What does attachment theory say about the relationship between early childhood attachment style and later adult relationships? Predict what David and Chelsea's adult relationships will be like based upon the descriptions of their attachment style.

THEORY COMPARISON QUESTIONS

1. How do attachment theories compare to object relations theories?

2. How could behaviorism explain the differences in David and Chelsea's attachment styles?

Case Study 16
John Bowlby and
Mary Ainsworth

Angela is about to break up with Justin after being in a relationship with him for five months. They met in college but their hometowns are in different states. They didn't have classes together. Instead, they met on a social networking site. She met him through one of her online friends and thought he looked cute in his photos on the site, so she contacted him. That is one of the great things about social networking sites according to Angela: Someone can meet another person that you normally wouldn't meet and start up a new friendship or relationship. She has met some really interesting people that way. In this case, Angela and Justin met online but eventually arranged to meet face-to-face once they found out they attended the same college. They met over lunch and seemed to hit it off. They started dating, and Angela thought Justin seemed sweet. He was eager to please and typically let Angela decide what to do on their dates. When they disagreed on what to do, Justin typically gave in to Angela's wishes. For example, one time they had agreed to go to a movie but when they arrived at the movie theater, both of them thought they were going to see different features. Justin told Angela that they could see the movie she wanted and that he'd see the other movie some other time.

Justin and Angela had been seeing each other for 10 weeks when the semester ended, and it was time to move back to their families' homes for the summer. That was the only time that Angela had met Justin's parents, and she was struck by just how different his parents were from hers. Justin's parents seemed cold and distant. They didn't seem excited to see him even though they hadn't seen him in four months. They interacted minimally with him, loaded up the car with Justin's belongings, and took off. Angela's parents, on the other hand, were eager to see their daughter again This was evident in the way their faces lit up when they first saw her and in the hugs and kisses they gave her when she greeted them. There weren't any hugs and kisses when Justin greeted his parents.

They were both sad to have to leave each other but each had summer jobs in their hometowns; they needed to work in order to pay for college the following year. They promised to talk on the phone and chat over the Internet and video conference. They also hoped to get together over the summer once or twice. Justin seemed more upset about their impending separation than Angela. He seemed close to tears and confessed that he was afraid that she would forget about him over the summer. She tried to reassure him but he didn't seem convinced. Eventually, they had to leave each other and go in different directions, promising each other that they would call on the road if they got the chance and, certainly, as soon as they got home.

Justin did indeed call Angela as soon as he got home. In fact, Angela was surprised at how soon he called because even though she had already arrived at her location also, she was busy catching up with her family about her life and theirs. Justin also called later that night just to say "good night." This pattern of calling each day at least twice continued for the next two weeks. Additionally, Justin suggested that they video conference because "he missed seeing her face." She agreed to the video conferencing because she liked the idea of seeing him also but then the hour video conferencing every couple of days became an everyday occurrence, along with the phone calls, and the hour video conferencing everyday became two hours everyday, in addition to the phone calls. At first the attention Justin gave Angela was flattering, but eventually it started to wear on her. She explained to him that she didn't have that much time to spend on video conferencing but Justin was hurt and claimed that she didn't really love him. She tried to reassure him that she was just busy but their conversations ended on a strained note. The next day, when Angela was on her social networking site with her friends, Justin messaged her and said he wanted to talk. Angela was a little annoyed because between her work schedule, spending time with her family, and talking to Justin, she had very little time to spend with her friends, but she accepted because she wanted to clear the air with Justin. Instead, the conversation turned into another argument with Justin accusing Angela of cheating on him. She denied it, explaining her busy schedule but again he seemed unconvinced. Justin agreed to give Angela some space. The next day he sent her flowers apologizing for his behavior but Angela was still annoyed. The space Justin promised Angela lasted only a week. Eventually Justin started becoming demanding again. He texted her several times a day and became angry when she didn't text him back. He left messages on her cell phone when she didn't take his calls. Sometimes the messages were angry and accusatory; sometimes they were depressing, with him crying about how she didn't love him anymore. Angela is fed up with Justin's jealousy and clingy behavior. She feels smothered by his demanding nature and overwhelmed by his neediness. She thinks the best thing to do is to end the relationship.

APPLICATION QUESTIONS

Using Bowlby and Ainsworth's attachment theory, explain Angela and Justin's behavior by answering the following questions.

1. According to Bowlby and Ainsworth, what type of adult attachment style does Justin appear to have? Angela? Explain.

2. According to attachment theory, how does childhood attachment style influence adult attachment style and adult relationships?

3. According to Bowlby and Ainsworth, what is the cause of Justin's maladjusted attachment style? What caused Angela's attachment style?

THEORY COMPARISON QUESTIONS

1. How does Bowlby and Ainsworth's theory compare to evolutionary psychological perspectives? How can it be seen as evolutionary psychology?

2. How does Horney's theory relate to attachment theory? How could Horney's theory explain Justin's clingy behavior?

Helpful Hints

Are you having a problem answering some of the application questions for Case 15 or 16? See if the following will help you.

Bowlby and Ainsworth suggested that the way we act in adult relationships is similar to the type of relationship we developed in childhood with our caregivers, especially our parents. If our parents are warm and nurturing, we develop a secure relationship with them. This is reflected in healthy adult relationships. If, however, we do not develop a secure relationship with

our caregivers, perhaps because they have difficulty showing us affection or are not responsive to our needs, we could develop an avoidant or ambivalent attachment style in childhood. This attachment style is then a model for later adult relationships. People with the avoidant attachment style have difficulty developing relationships and can be described as loners, whereas people with the ambivalent attachment style can be described as clingy, always concerned that their partners/friends really do not care about them.

Abraham Maslow (1908–1970)

Holistic Dynamic Theory
Why learn this theory?

Contributions

While his theory can explain maladjustment, Maslow's primary emphasis was on understanding psychologically healthy people. Although he saw the benefits of both behaviorism and psychoanalysis Maslow also criticized them, suggesting that they emphasized the unhealthy personality too much and that they had a limited understanding of adjustment. In his view, these schools of thought did not allow the psychologist to view the human being completely. Maslow's holistic-dynamic theory, in contrast, took a holistic approach to understanding human behavior, suggesting that we are all motivated by a variety of needs at any given time. These needs could be either physiological or psychological in nature. Thus, his hierarchy of needs is one of his most important contributions to the field of psychology, resulting in the development of a third school of thought (besides behaviorism and psychoanalysis): humanism. The needs hierarchy is useful, not just in the field of psychology but also in business, where it is widely applied and discussed in management theory. Additionally, although Jung first described self-realization, an idea similar to actualization, it was Maslow who really popularized this concept. Maslow saw actualization, a human striving to pursue their highest potential, as vital in the pursuit of human happiness and adjustment. In sum, Abraham Maslow is considered a founder of humanistic psychology and popularized its values, encouraging growth, happiness, and adjustment in all people.

Case Study 17
Abraham Maslow

Cindy is a four-year-old who has had a troubling early childhood. She was taken away from her parents and placed in a foster home when she was only six months old after her pediatrician contacted Children and Youth Services because she was concerned that Cindy was being neglected. When the pediatrician first saw Cindy (and on subsequent occasions), the child appeared unkempt and had an odor that suggested that she had not been washed recently. Likewise, the physician was also concerned about neglect because of Cindy's lack of growth. At the first checkup, which usually occurs when a baby is about two weeks old, Cindy had not gained a sufficient amount of weight. Babies usually lose a few ounces during their stay in the hospital, but they are expected to regain that weight (and sometimes more) by the time they are two weeks old. Cindy was four weeks old at her first checkup and had gained back the weight she had lost in the hospital but had not put on any additional weight. Cindy had also not gained adequate weight at her six-week checkup (which actually occurred at nine weeks). It did not appear that physical reasons were the cause of the lack of growth. Rather, when the pediatrician asked how much formula the baby was given, the answer indicated it was not an adequate amount. The physician reprimanded the adult with Cindy (her grandmother) and instructed her on the amount of formula that is necessary for a child that age. However, at her three-month checkup, which was also late, Cindy still was not growing adequately. At this third visit, Cindy also had a terrible diaper rash. Her skin was so raw that in some places it was raised up, indicating a yeast infection. The severity of the diaper rash alarmed the pediatrician. Usually parents brought their babies in before a diaper rash became that bad (or treated it themselves before it progressed to this point), but the physician hadn't even met the parents. Instead, Cindy's maternal grandmother had brought her in on each occasion. The woman was quite elderly with severe arthritis, but she made the effort to bring Cindy in because of the diaper rash. Although the grandmother was not Cindy's guardian, she thought it was important for the child to receive the usual immunization shots and to be checked periodically by a physician—that is, whenever the grandmother was physically able to make the visits. Cindy's guardian was actually her mother. When the pediatrician asked why the mother did not accompany Cindy to these visits, the grandmother was vague and said that she was not available. The physician therefore suspected that Cindy was being neglected by her mother. She did not seem to be receiving adequate nutrition or hygiene.

When Children and Youth Services personnel investigated, they found that Cindy was born to a 40-year-old mother who was a drug addict and who had no interest in rehabilitation. She was a single mother who did not have a home of her own but instead lived with friends. These friends lived in a relatively poor neighborhood that housed primarily African-Americans and Latinos. Cindy and her mother were also African-American. They would live at one friend's place for a time and then move on to another friend who would put them up for a while. Occasionally, they would visit and live with Cindy's grandmother. On these occasions, the grandmother brought Cindy to the pediatrician but Cindy's grandmother was elderly and sickly and so could not take care of the strenuous physical needs of an infant. No one knew who Cindy's father was, and there were no other relatives.

Although Children and Youth Services attempted to intervene on Cindy's behalf with her mother by providing education and parent training, her mother's drug addiction prevented adequate care. On one occasion when the caseworker visited Cindy and her mother, Cindy was so severely dehydrated that she was in medical danger. When asked about the cause, Cindy's mother replied that it was "just the flu" and that medical attention was not needed. When pressed, Cindy's mother refused to take her to a doctor or hospital, stating that she did not have the money to do so. In actuality, Cindy's mother was in need of a fix and preferred to use the money for that. So, Cindy was placed in a foster home.

Although there are many loving foster homes, Cindy unfortunately was placed in one where she received adequate nutrition, physical care, and shelter but little else. Her foster family was more concerned about receiving adequate compensation for their foster care than they were with the welfare of the child. Her foster parents showed her little affection, rarely holding her or talking to her. Over the course of a few months, the neighborhood in which she and her foster family lived deteriorated, and gang violence, including drive-by shootings, began. The foster family decided to move to another state and did not want to adopt Cindy. Her caseworker was notified, and Cindy was to be placed with another foster family. Contact with Cindy's biological mother was sporadic, and Cindy could not be placed back with her mother because of the mother's continued drug addiction.

At the age of 12 months, Cindy looked as though she was only 6 months old, and although she could sit up on her own, she still hadn't started to crawl, let alone walk. She cringed at someone's touch, having gotten very little during her first year of life. She also seemed very shy and uncertain of herself. She became frightened and cried easily. Although Cindy's material needs were met, her lack of interaction with people and the absence of love from her foster and biological families did not allow her to thrive.

The caseworker placed Cindy with another foster family. Fortunately for Cindy, this family was very caring. They lived in a clean, quiet, working-class neighborhood where other small children were being raised. Her new foster mother stayed home with Cindy and her two biological daughters, ages five and eight, during the day; she also worked part time at a catalog company taking orders over the phone four evenings a week after her husband came home. Cindy's new foster father worked as a supervisor at a warehouse that distributed nonfood items to supermarkets. Both foster parents were very patient and showed affection readily. Their two daughters were thrilled to have a baby sister to help take care of. Although Cindy was very tentative at first, she gradually began to seek out physical contact, especially when she was frightened or not feeling well. Within eight weeks, Cindy had grown and developed enough to look like a nine-month-old. Within six months, Cindy had caught up developmentally and physically with other children her age. During this time, Cindy's mother overdosed and died. Because no other family members were willing or able to take care of Cindy, she was put up for adoption. Fortunately for Cindy, her foster family members had grown to love her so much that they applied to adopt her and were granted their request. Cindy now lives with her adopted family and is a happy, confident, four-year-old.

APPLICATION QUESTIONS

Using Maslow's holistic dynamic theory, analyze Cindy's life by answering the following questions.

1. Consider Maslow's hierarchy of needs during Cindy's first year of life. Which needs were fulfilled? Which were not?

2. What was the outcome of the needs being fulfilled or not fulfilled?

3. Which of Maslow's needs were fulfilled for Cindy during her second year of life? What was the outcome of that?

4. What type of values would Cindy have to embrace in order to actualize?

THEORY COMPARISON QUESTIONS

1. How do Maslow's safety needs compare with Erikson's concepts of learning basic trust in the oral sensory stage? Apply this concept to Cindy's

experience, explaining what crisis can lead to basic trust and whether it was developed for Cindy.

2. How do Sullivan's concepts of needs differ from Maslow's? Which of Sullivan's needs were met for Cindy before and after her adoption? Which were not?

3. How does Horney's concept of basic anxiety compare with Maslow's safety needs and love needs? Apply this concept to Cindy's experiences before and after her adoption.

Case Study 18
Abraham Maslow

Frank is a 42-year-old, Native American, married factory worker with two children. He lives in a small town in western Pennsylvania that is located about an hour away from the nearest major city. The factory he works at manufactures chairs. He has been working the graveyard shift (11 P.M. to 7 A.M.) for about six years now. The hours are terrible, and he has never really gotten used to them. He tries to sleep when he gets home in the early morning but finds it difficult because his children are getting ready for school at that time and his wife is getting ready for work. Even if he waits to go to bed until everyone leaves the house, Frank still has trouble sleeping in the daytime. He is tired all the time, but at least he gets some sleep on weekends, and the money earned working the third shift is better than that for the first or second shift. Sometimes he thinks that if he could just get enough sleep, he would be a truly happy man.

Between their two incomes, Frank and his wife have been able to support their family. They have been able to buy a small house; there is always food on the table, and their children have decent clothes to wear. The house, the clothes, and the food are not fancy but always adequate. That is, Frank and his wife have been able to support their family until recently. Frank has just lost his job. Frank's plant had been bought out by a rival out-of-state company, and initially there seemed to be no change in the production schedule. Then one Friday, Frank received a notice in his paycheck telling him that this was his last day of work and asking him to take all of his personal belongings with him. The factory was to be closed immediately because of the buyout. Frank was devastated by the news, as were his coworkers.

The workers were also surprised by the news. It seemed as though the chair company had always been there, and they thought it always would be. Their fathers had worked at, and retired from, the company. Some of the workers' grandfathers did too. They thought that their jobs were secure. They were wrong.

Frank and his coworkers had always taken pride in their work. They crafted their chairs by hand, using tools their fathers had used before them. They produced an excellent product. Frank was especially proud of the intricate designs he made on the backs of the chairs he produced. His skill earned him the respect of his coworkers. Now, two months after the closing, Frank is not proud of very much. He has not been able to find any other work, and he is embarrassed by the prospect of not being able to support his family. Although he and his wife have been able to make ends meet temporarily because of her job and his unemployment compensation, he is not sure what will happen when his unemployment compensation runs out. How will they pay their mortgage? How will they put food on the table? How could they possibly save for their retirement?

Depending on his wife's income has been especially hard on Frank. He believes that he should be the breadwinner, but his wife has been incredibly supportive since the plant closing. She is constantly trying to boost his self-esteem and has never complained once about the things they have had to give up. He loves her very much and wishes he could do more for her and for his children, whom he adores. He would give anything to go back to being tired all the time, if he could have his job back. He feels useless and incompetent.

APPLICATION QUESTIONS

Using Maslow's holistic dynamic theory, analyze Frank's life by answering the following questions.

1. Which of Maslow's needs, described in his hierarchy, were met for Frank before he was laid off? Provide examples and explain.

2. Which needs were not met before Frank was laid off? Explain.

3. Which of Maslow's needs were met for Frank after he was laid off? Provide examples and explain.

4. Which needs were not met after Frank was laid off? Explain.

THEORY COMPARISON QUESTIONS

1. How do Maslow's needs compare with those discussed by Rogers? Which of Rogers' needs were met for Frank before he was laid off? After he was laid off?

2. How do the needs of Maslow compare with those discussed by Fromm? Which of Fromm's needs were met for Frank before he was laid off? After he was laid off?

3. How could Kelly's modulation corollary and the concept of permeability explain Frank's feelings of uselessness and incompetence after the loss of his job? How does the focus of Kelly's theory differ from that of Maslow's?

Helpful Hints

Are you having a problem answering some of the application questions for Case 17 or 18? See if the following will help you.

Maslow's theory is a fairly straightforward one, but keep in mind a couple of points. First, needs are not always met completely and may not be met totally before the next need in the hierarchy becomes significant. For example, we all occasionally ignore fatigue or hunger in order to fulfill our many obligations that, most likely, involve other needs higher up in the hierarchy, but our physiological needs are met partially and to a satisfactory level. Also, keep in mind that not everyone will strive for actualization. Those who do are motivated by B motivation (or needs), also referred to as *metamotivation* and Being values. Those who do not work toward actualization are influenced by D (deficiency) needs or values. Finally, actualization is not something that is attained completely but rather worked toward continually.

Carl Rogers (1902–1987)

Person-Centered Theory
Why learn this theory?

Contributions

Carl Rogers is known for being one of the founders of humanistic psychology, and he deeply influenced the world with his work and his writing. His contributions are numerous and reach far beyond just the field of psychology and psychotherapy, influencing, for example, the fields of education and peace and conflict resolution. Rogers' concept of unconditional positive regard, our need to be accepted in nonjudgmental ways, is especially relevant to many fields and was central in the development of a new approach to therapy: Rogers' person-centered psychotherapy.

Like Maslow, Rogers popularized the notion of actualization, although his conceptualization of the term was different from that of Maslow. For Rogers, actualization was a matter of becoming a fully functioning person. He observed that in order for someone to become fully functioning, certain conditions must be met. Thus, Rogers was instrumental in developing our understanding of the factors contributing to adjustment, including unconditional positive regard, and of the factors contributing to maladjustment, including conditions of worth. Conditions of worth is an especially relevant concept because so many of us try to live up to other people's expectations in order to gain their approval and affection. We engage in behaviors (e.g., choose careers, majors, colleges) because *others* want us to, because of pressure from others, not because *we* want to. Living up to other people's expectations denies us the ability to do what we desire. It denies us the ability to develop our own interests. Rogers called attention to this tendency and encouraged people to be true to themselves, thereby promoting growth and adjustment.

Case Study 19
Carl Rogers

K atharine is scheduled to attend her 20th high school reunion next month and is looking forward to it. She missed her 10th high school reunion purposely because she had felt like such a failure. She was afraid that her old classmates would have accomplished much more than she had. Even worse, she was afraid that they would feel sorry for her.

Just before her 10th reunion, Katharine was divorced, and she was working as a secretary to support herself. Katharine had married her high school sweetheart the year after they graduated. She had always wanted to be married; as a child, she dreamt of it. So, when her boyfriend asked her to marry him, she happily agreed. But marriage was not everything she had hoped it would be. In high school she had dreams of also owning her own business, but her husband disapproved of her taking business courses at the local community college and discouraged any attempts she made at earning money on her own. He wanted a wife who stayed home and took care of him and his house. The marriage was disappointing also because even though they tried, she had been unable to become pregnant. The marriage ended when her husband began an affair with a coworker and asked Katharine for a divorce so that he could marry his new love. Katharine was devastated.

She had no husband, no children, and no career. She had never imagined herself in that situation. In high school, she had always thought she would be one of those women who had it all: a career and family life. Now she was a secretary in someone else's business with no family possibilities in sight. To make matters worse, Katharine had gained 30 pounds the year after she was divorced. She had always been slender and had no intentions of going to her reunion looking the way she now did.

A coworker noted Katharine's depression after her divorce and suggested that she accompany her to her women's support group. The support group changed Katharine's life. The other women in the group listened to what she said and seemed to understand what she was going through. As she continued to go to the group, and as she learned that they would not pity her or make fun of her, she opened up more and discussed her feelings. Eventually she told them about her high school dream of owning her own business. She had been reluctant to discuss this with them at first because her ex-husband had always made fun of her when she brought up the possibility. Instead of criticism, she received support from her group.

They encouraged her to take a few business courses and discussed with her what type of business she could open. When they found out that she was artistic, they suggested that she try making and selling some crafts at various craft shows. Katharine did just that, experimenting with various floral arrangements, Christmas decorations, and knickknacks on weekends and evenings. Although these items sold, she did not sell enough of them to be able to support herself and start her own business. She didn't find her niche until she started woodworking. She began making Victorian-looking Santas out of wood and hand painting them. They had Katharine's own unique touches. She was surprised to sell out her inventory on the second day of a three-day craft show. This gave her the confidence she needed.

Katharine built up her inventory and rented a small storefront where she began to sell her Santas along with other commissioned handmade items from other artisans with whom she had networked. Eventually, she was making enough money to be able to quit her secretarial job and devote all of her attention to her business. Her items became so popular that she had to employ two other people part time to organize her inventory and fill online orders that she received from the website she had developed advertising her product and business.

Opening her business had other positive effects as well. It had kept her so busy that she did not always have time to eat, so Katharine lost 20 of the 30 pounds she had gained after her divorce. Socially, she saw more people such as her "regulars," customers who came back repeatedly and collected her Santas. In fact, one customer she met at her shop (also a wood-worker) asked her out, and their relationship had blossomed to the extent that they married. She also felt needed because she had two coworkers who depended on her. She depended on them as well, and they occasionally came up with good suggestions for the store and the website, and their handling of the inventory and website orders allowed Katharine more time to craft her Santas. She even became active in the local chamber of commerce. Katharine no longer feels like a failure and is confident about attending her 20th reunion.

APPLICATION QUESTIONS

Using Rogers' person-centered theory, explain Katherine's behavior by answering the following questions.

1. How did Katharine's self-concept differ from her ideal self before her experience with her support group? What does this imply about her mental health, according to Rogers' theory?

2. How could Rogers' theory explain the cause of any difference in Katharine's selves?

3. How did Katharine's self-concept differ from her ideal self after her experience with her support group? What does this imply about her mental health, according to Rogers' theory?

4. What Rogerian therapist characteristics did Katherine's support group provide that allowed for a decrease in incongruence among her selves?

THEORY COMPARISON QUESTIONS

1. What other theories, besides Rogers', could be applied to Katherine's experiences to explain them? How?

2. Apply Bandura's concepts of self-regulation and self-efficacy to Katherine's experiences. How does the focus of Bandura's theory differ from that of Rogers'?

3. How do the needs discussed by Rogers compare with those discussed by Fromm? By Maslow?

4. Use May's concepts of responsibility and authenticity to explain Katherine's lifestyle changes.

Case Study 20
Carl Rogers

Allen works assembling cars at a local General Motors (GM) plant near his home. His job is a good one: he earns a decent salary, has help from the company for purchasing such benefits as health insurance and retirement, and his supervisor treats him and his coworkers well, asking their opinions about how to make their work run more smoothly and efficiently. As he approaches the age of 30, however, he has become increasingly dissatisfied with his work life. He wishes that he could do something more fulfilling and meaningful.

When he was younger, Allen dreamed of becoming a teacher. He was quite a good student in grade school and high school and had always loved children. Even as a child himself, Allen loved to play with the younger children on his street, and they loved to play with him. During the summer, the younger children would come down to his house and Allen would construct elaborate scenarios for them to act out. They would play pirates, or cops and robbers, or have pretend medieval jousting matches. In high school, Allen had decided to attend college and become a grade school teacher.

Allen's family was a typical working-class family. They had not been rich, but they had a decent home and enough food on the table and clothes on their backs. Although his parents did not really understand why Allen wanted to go to college, they preferred that he would just find a decent job and settle down. They loved him and agreed to help him pay for tuition at the local college to help him fulfill his dream of becoming a teacher. Allen applied for admission to the college and was accepted. He completed one semester but in the middle of that semester, his younger brother became very ill and required extensive medical treatment. Although Allen's father had some health insurance, it was not adequate to cover the considerable medical bills. His parents told Allen that they would not be able to pay for his tuition anymore and pressured him into finding a job and contributing to the family financially. Under a great deal of stress, both Allen's father and mother expressed the notions that they thought that college was a waste of time and money, an excuse to not settle down and work. Luckily for Allen, the GM plant was just opening in his area. He applied for a position and was hired. A dutiful son, Allen, who was living at home, contributed part of his paycheck to his family to pay for his brother's medical expenses. His parents had always emphasized the importance of taking care of family when he was growing up and that was what Allen was trying to do.

A few months after beginning his job at the assembly plant, Allen's girlfriend, whom he had started dating in high school, became pregnant. Although they were careful, contraception does not work 100 percent effectively, and Allen and his girlfriend, Sue, had to make a decision about the pregnancy. Neither wanted to abort the child. Furthermore, Allen knew his parents would be very disapproving, perhaps even disowning him, if he did not support and care for his child, and he was willing to do so. Because they loved each other and had been seeing each other for almost three years, Sue and Allen decided to get married. Their parents helped them with the expense of the wedding and setting up their own household. Although their parents would have preferred that the pregnancy come after the marriage, both sets of parents were thrilled with the prospect of becoming grandparents.

Allen and Sue set up house in a small apartment. It was comfortable, though sparsely furnished. Between Allen's salary and Sue's income as a part-time cashier at one of the local supermarkets, they were able to make ends meet and save a little money toward a down payment for a house. Sue quit her job to stay home with the baby, and Allen worked the occasional overtime to continue to earn enough to pay bills and save for a house. Eventually, they were able to buy a house and soon had another baby.

Allen was thrilled to be a father because he always had loved children. He was an affectionate father, a loving spouse, and a good provider. Supporting and caring for his family was important to him. But now, having been married for about 10 years, having his children in school, and approaching his 30th birthday, Allen feels some discontentment and anxiety. He wonders if there is anything else in life. He feels that if he is going to accomplish anything else, he needs to begin to work toward it now. And, he wonders if he should go back to school to earn his degree and get a job as a teacher. Sue was about to go back to work. With the children in school now, she could work full time and have the grandparents mind the children after school. The money she would earn could be used to send Allen to college. But whenever Allen brings up the possibility of using the money to go back to school, Sue replies that the money could be used for better things than sending him to college, things like a new roof, new windows, a paved driveway, and better furniture. She does not understand why he would want to give up his job at the plant with its salary and benefits to find a job as a teacher. He is good at what he does. Allen's parents reiterate the same sentiments.

Besides talking to his wife and parents about his idea of becoming a teacher, Allen has tried to talk to some of his coworkers about it. They don't understand either. They think he would be crazy to give up his job. Good jobs are hard to come by. This isn't the first time Allen wasn't understood by his coworkers. Allen, who has always loved to read, would often read books or magazine articles during breaks, and he would sometimes try to discuss them at work. His coworkers' responses were not very favorable, and sometimes they would laugh at some of the ideas he would bring up. Although they liked Allen, they thought he was a little weird sometimes. Allen sometimes wondered if he was weird too. He didn't seem to fit in at work, and his wife and parents did not understand him. He sometimes felt that he wasn't who everybody thought he was. He thought he was a good worker, a good father, and a good husband, and that was how everyone else saw him as well. Allen, however, also saw himself as a college student, teacher, and mentor to children. He wished he could become that. He was proud of who he was now but that was not who he wanted to be.

Lately, Allen has been talking to one coworker over lunch and breaks. Although most of his coworkers laugh at his ideas or tell him they do not understand him, this one listens and supports him. Allen could say anything to this coworker and not be afraid of being laughed at or criticized. This coworker, who years ago had had thoughts similar to Allen's, seemed to know exactly what he was going through and helped him see things more clearly. Sometimes the coworker would repeat what Allen just said in a slightly different way, and Allen would suddenly have an insight. He felt as though he was growing as a person. Allen looked forward to these talks. They strengthened his resolve about becoming a teacher. He hopes that his parents and his wife will accept him as he wants to be and support his decision.

APPLICATION QUESTIONS

Using Rogers' person-centered theory, explain Allen's behavior by answering the following questions.

1. Which of Rogers' needs are fulfilled for Allen? Which are not met? Explain.
2. How does Allen's perceived self differ from his ideal self?
3. Why would Allen's perceived self be different than his ideal self?
4. The coworker with whom Allen talks at lunch and breaks shares the characteristics of a Rogerian therapist. List them and explain how the coworker displays them.
5. What would Allen have to do to actualize?

THEORY COMPARISON QUESTIONS

1. "Apply Bandura's concept of reciprocal determinism to Allen's experiences."? How does the environmental factor in reciprocal determinism compare with Rogers' unconditional positive regard?

2. How could Skinner's radical behaviorism explain Allen's ambition to change careers? How does the focus of Skinner's theory compare with that of Rogers' theory?

3. How does Erikson's concept of identity, formed during the adolescent stage, apply to Allen's ambition to change careers? How does it compare with Rogers' self-concept?

Helpful Hints

Are you having a problem answering some of the application questions for Case 19 or 20? See if the following will help you.

One of the most confusing aspects of Rogers' theory deals with the self structure. He discusses an organismic self, a perceived self, and an ideal self. The organismic self is the total self that includes both the perceived self and the ideal self, but it also contains other aspects of the self of which we are unaware. The perceived self is who we think we are (which may or may not be accurate). The ideal self is what we would like to be like. There isn't much discrepancy between the ideal and perceived self in someone who is well adjusted. Similarly, the actualization tendency and the self-actualization tendency are almost identical in a mentally healthy person. Self-actualization is the tendency to actualize the perceived self and is a subsystem of the (more general) actualization tendency. The actualization tendency refers to actualizing the *entire* organism: conscious and unconscious, physical and psychological. If these two tendencies are discrepant (incongruent), a person is attempting to become something they are not, that is, their organismic experience is different from their self-concept. The greater the discrepancy, the greater the maladjustment. This most likely results from conditions of worth.

Rollo May (1909–1994)

Existential Analytic Theory
Why learn this theory?

Contributions

Rollo May is often referred to as the Father of American Existential Psychology. Existential psychology first began in Europe and was rooted in such philosophical writings of Jean-Paul Satre and Friedrich Nietzsche, among others, but it was May who promoted the ideas of existentialism in the United States. May was a keen observer of the human condition and is best known for his writings on anxiety, creativity, and for integrating the field of psychology with the arts.

May is well known for helping people to develop their own sense of selves and to live authentically, through the development of his existential psychotherapy and through the publication of numerous books that millions of people in the general public read. Thus, not only did May contribute to the field of personality psychology, he touched the lives of millions of people outside the field of psychology. Throughout his writings he encouraged people to grow and be responsible for their own lives. He thought that many people give up their freedom by allowing others to make decisions and choices for them. In particular, he thought that many people unknowingly conform to others' expectations and that this conformity does not allow people to live authentically. These ideas were reiterated by Carl Rogers who discussed conditions of worth (engaging in behaviors in order to gain others' approval or love) and the necessity to actualize the real self, not an inaccurate version of the perceived self.

In sum, May sent a message that suggested that we have control over who we are and what our lives are like. That message further suggested that if we are unhappy, if we feel alienated, we are responsible for making changes that will make us happier. He encouraged people to find the courage to live according to their own value system and to engage in behaviors that they find meaningful.

Case Study 21
Rollo May

Jillian is a Caucasian, 33-year-old lesbian, a successful writer for a popular news magazine. She got married in one of the thousands of ceremonies held in San Francisco during 2004 when courts in a number of cities defied laws and allowed same-sex couples to marry. She is about to give birth to a baby she conceived through in vitro fertilization. She has both gay and straight friends. Life is good, but it hasn't always seemed that way. For years Jillian struggled with her sexual orientation and the painful process of coming out whereby someone who is gay or lesbian accepts that they are homosexual and no longer wants to hide that fact.

As a child, Jillian always felt a bit different from the other children. She didn't know why until sometime during her college experience. As a teenager her friends fawned over pictures and articles of young male rock stars or movie or television actors, but Jillian noticed that she wasn't really interested in them, although she pretended to be in order to fit in with her friends. Instead, Jillian noticed the females whom those male stars were with and found that she was attracted to them. At first she ignored those feelings of attraction, and she occasionally dated boys in high school. But she was never very interested in them, physically or emotionally. The same was true in college: she dated, but had difficulty forming a lasting relationship with a man. During her junior year in college, she began to feel that she was incapable of falling in love, and although she had heterosexual sex with her dates, she found that she could get aroused only if she imagined that she was with another woman. She wondered what was wrong with her. Her girlfriends seemed to be able to fall in and out of love all the time, and the stories they told about their sex lives made her uncomfortable because they seemed to enjoy the act so much more than she did.

Then at the age of 22 when she was working on her master's degree, she met another female graduate student, Erin, with whom she instantly bonded. Erin and Jillian became best friends, taking in movies, going to bars on the weekend, visiting the beach. They both had a lot in common: their interest in writing and their love of racquetball, rollerblading, and dogs. As their friendship grew, Jillian found she could no longer deny to herself that she was in love with her best friend. The relationship was platonic, and Jillian never professed her love to Erin, out of fear that Erin would be repulsed and would break off their friendship. Jillian sought out a therapist, again thinking that there was something wrong with her. But after a minimal number of sessions the therapist broached the possibility that Jillian was lesbian. Initially Jillian was resistant to the idea. She had never known someone who was gay and Jillian had never thought of herself as lesbian before, but now that she was in love she was able to understand and put her other dating experiences into perspective. Her therapist helped Jillian to accept her homosexuality. Jillian still did not profess her love to Erin, and when they earned their master's degrees, they parted ways but still kept in touch through e-mail and phone calls.

Jillian also had trouble telling others about her homosexuality. She was afraid of their reactions, but at the age of 27, she got tired of hiding her sexual orientation. She was tired of coming up with excuses to not date men, tired of being asked when she was going to get married, and tired of feeling like she was living a lie. She decided to take a chance and tell her brother, Adam, with whom she had always been close, about being lesbian. His initial reaction was surprise but he quickly came around, gave her a hug, and told her that the only thing that mattered was that she was happy. He even cracked a joke by telling her that he'd stop fixing her up with his friends. Jillian felt intense relief and got a bit teary-eyed by his support. Bolstered by her success, she decided to tell her parents. That experience was not as positive as the one with her brother, but could have been worse. Her parents were in denial for a period of time. They suggested that Jillian see a therapist, that she could change her sexual orientation. They fretted about her never getting married or having children. Some of the reactions of her friends were supportive; others felt so negatively about homosexuality that they eventually stopped interacting with Jillian. Unfortunately, Erin was one of those who reacted negatively to Jillian's news. While the loss of relationships saddened Jillian, every time she came out to someone she cared about, she felt an immense sense of relief. She no longer felt like she was hiding something.

Jillian was happy and satisfied with her coming out. Although it took quite a while, she was comfortable with her sexual orientation and her openness. Eventually, Jillian made contact with a couple of gay and lesbian organizations, and she met and dated other women. But it wasn't until she met Anana, an African American lesbian who worked as an activist for one of those organizations that she finally formed a long-term serious relationship. She felt happy, but the one thing that bothered Jillian about her sexual orientation was not having children.

When Jillian was 31, she started feeling as though her biological clock was ticking. At times she felt bitter: Heterosexuals who were in long-term relationships could marry and produce children. But for Jillian and Anana, life was more complex. Although they wanted to marry, it was against the law, and although they both wanted to be mothers, they physically could not produce a child without assistance. After a lot of talking, Jillian and Anana decided to try to have a child despite the legal limitations of their sexual orientation. To make them feel as though both would be the child's mother, they decided to use Anana's ova for the fertilization procedure, but the blastocyst (fertilized egg) would be placed in Jillian, who would then carry the baby to term. They were lucky; not all in vitro fertilization procedures work the first time, but, for them, it did. It seemed like a sign that they had done the right thing. They did fret about what would happen to their child if one of them died: would the other be given custody or would there be some sort of court battle over who would raise the child? What would happen to the remaining partner financially if one of them died? How could they provide for their child? Their places of employment did not acknowledge lesbians as married couples no matter how long they lived together. They planned on making legal provisions in the event something like this happened, but still it was a concern, a concern that married heterosexual couples did not have to face. Then, surprisingly, gay and lesbian couples began to get married in San Francisco. They took this as another fortuitous sign and decided to get married also. Jillian was six months pregnant but both she and Anana waited in long lines for the event. Both held roses, their favorite flower, to represent love during the ceremony. Although there are still court challenges to the legality of their marriage, they see it as a binding contract.

APPLICATION QUESTIONS

Using May's existential analytic theory, analyze Jillian's behavior by answering the following questions.

1. What is May's concept of the human dilemma? Find an example of it in the case study.

2. Assume that homosexuality has a physical cause.★ Use the three modes of existence and the concept of alienation to explain Jillian's experience with her sexual orientation.

3. Use May's concepts of responsibility and authenticity to explain Jillian's decisions to come out, to have a child, and to get married.

4. Define May's four types of love. Which type of love best illustrates Jillian's relationship with Erin? With her brother? With Anana? With her baby?

★Author's note: There are many theories that explain homosexuality. Some embrace physical causes, others environmental. Right now there appears to be more support for the physical (e.g., genetics, brain differences) than for environmental causes. At least, that is where a lot of research is being conducted, as you may have heard about in the mass media, but there is no definitive explanation. For the sake of learning some of May's concepts, assume that the cause is physical.

THEORY COMPARISON QUESTIONS

1. How is May's concept of the human dilemma different from Fromm's concept with the same name?

2. Compare and contrast May's concept of alienation with Rogers' concepts of conditions of worth and incongruence.

Case Study 22
Rollo May

Camille is a 31-year-old single woman in therapy for extreme shyness, a mild form of social phobia. She would like to get married and have children but knew she would not be able to do so without therapy to overcome her shyness. Her 30th birthday and her biological clock prompted her to seek therapy even though her family disapproved of the prospect. At that point, however, Camille was discouraged by her shyness and lonely enough to risk familial disapproval in the hopes that therapy would alleviate the anxious feelings she had whenever she tried to interact with another person. Like many people, Camille doesn't know what to say when she first meets someone, but, for her, the interaction is much more stressful than for others who are just mildly shy. Camille's palms sweat; her mouth feels dry; and she feels as though she is being judged poorly by everyone, even those she is meeting for the first time. She is afraid that she is making a terrible first impression. Even making telephone calls, including placing a food takeout order, creates anxiety for her, because, again, she feels as though she is being judged.

Camille has no friends, and although she has a job in an office, she has minimal interactions with coworkers. Coworkers often describe her as difficult to talk to. When they attempt to strike up a conversation with her, she listens to them but doesn't respond, not because she is unfriendly or dislikes them, but rather because she is at a loss for words. Unfortunately, her verbal reticence is interpreted as disinterest and she is left to eat lunch alone, even though she longs to join others. Even in occasional holiday family gatherings, where she is surrounded by people she has known all her life, Camille is silent.

This silence most likely began during childhood, as she was raised on the premise that children were seen and not heard. Both her parents were quite authoritarian, and her mother was especially critical. If Camille would ask a question, her mother would answer in such a way that made Camille feel stupid and implied that she should have known the answer. If she picked out her clothes herself, her mother would tell her what a poor choice in matching clothes she made. If Camille did not respond well to her mother's belittling jokes, it was Camille who didn't have a sense of humor. The few friends she did have were so uncomfortable at her house, because of her parents' strict rules and her mother's critical nature, that they eventually stopped coming. She modeled some of her mother's judgmental mannerisms, thinking that they were the correct ways to behave, but instead they further ostracized her from her peers. Eventually Camille grew up unsure of her feelings, socially unskilled, and with a sense of inferiority.

During the course of therapy, she realized that her silence was probably a way of protecting herself from the perpetual criticism she encountered during childhood. She also became aware of the parenting style to which she was exposed and of which she had never been aware. Camille thought that her experiences as a child were the same as everyone else's until she discovered during a group session that other children were raised differently, by parents who were not as strict or rigid and who were more patient, more understanding, and not as critical. Up until this point Camille idolized her parents, especially her mother, thinking that a strict upbringing was what children needed to develop into responsible adults. But this adoration most likely developed because her mother had always portrayed herself positively as a martyr who worked hard to take care of her family. Her mother had a tendency to tell the family about compliments she might have gotten, but shrewdly failed to let on that anyone might feel negatively about her. When friendships were lost or family relationships became sour, it was always the other party's fault, and Camille's mother was the victim. Beyond this, because Camille rarely interacted with her peers, she had no comparison point for her parents or their parenting style. She therefore assumed that the interactions she had while growing up were normal and typical.

During therapy sessions, not only did Camille examine her childhood experiences with her parents, she also made progress in decreasing some of the anxiety she felt during interpersonal interactions. In addition, talking during therapy helped Camille develop her social skills. Camille made so much progress during therapy that, even though she still felt somewhat shy and nervous about meeting other people, she brought up the possibility of joining a dating service. She knew that her parents would disapprove, having listened to them make statements about only losers joining such organizations. But since her coworkers were primarily female and since she did not especially like going to bars to meet men, Camille thought that a dating service might be an alternative way to meet potential dates. With her therapist's support, she did join a dating service and is beginning to date. She still feels quite nervous before the dates but the anxiety isn't as bad as it used to be. Her therapist also suggested that she start some type of volunteer work to meet same-sex friends. Again her parents were disapproving, indicating that it didn't make sense to work for no pay. But again Camille decided to take the chance. Although she still needs additional work on social skills and still needs to decrease her social anxiety, Camille is making progress in alleviating some of her symptoms of social phobia.

APPLICATION QUESTIONS

Using May's existential analytic theory, analyze Camille's behavior by answering the following questions.

1. Use May's three modes of existence and his concept of alienation to explain Camille's lack of relationships.

2. Use May's concepts of responsibility and authenticity to explain Camille's decisions to get therapy and join a dating service.

3. What is the primary task of the therapist, according to May? Find an example that illustrates it in the case.

4. What is neurotic anxiety, according to May? Find an example of it in the case.

THEORY COMPARISON QUESTIONS

1. Compare and contrast Rogers' concept of congruency and May's concept of authenticity.

2. How can behaviorism explain Camille's social phobia?

3. Compare and contrast Fromm's concept of the human dilemma to that of May.

4. How could attachment theory view social phobia?

Helpful Hints

Are you having a problem answering some of the application questions for Case 21 or 22? See if the following will help you.

For May, the human dilemma is the idea that we can see ourselves both subjectively and objectively. We can see things happening to us and, at the same time, we can experience those events. These events fall into three different modes of existence: the *umwelt,* the *mitwelt,* and the *eigenwelt. Umwelt* is the physical aspect of existence. *Mitwelt* is the sphere of personal relationships. *Eigenwelt* is a person's consciousness. Alienation is feeling separate from any of these three modes of existence, that is, from your physical nature,

from other people, or from yourself. It makes sense that May discussed these different aspects of our lives because humanists and existentialists are concerned with the whole person, as opposed to just certain aspects of the individual.

Humanists and existentialists also emphasize the potential for growth. Indeed, May suggested that we all are *responsible* for who we are and what we become. In other words, we control what our lives are like. Thus, we choose to either conform to others' or to society's expectations or we choose to live in a way that is valuable to ourselves. *Authenticity* is living one's life according to one's own value system.

George Kelly (1905–1967)

Personal Construct Theory
Why learn this theory?

Contributions

George Kelly is known for his personal construct theory, which suggests that people's behavior is determined by their interpretation and understanding of the world, that is, their constructs. Constructs are very similar to the more recent and more popular hypothetical structures known as schema, but constructs reflect how we see similarities and differences between things or people, whereas schema do not necessarily do so. Kelly thought that people behave as scientists, testing theories and revising them as necessary. He therefore suggested that constructs are subject to revision, and healthy people are able to change their views of the world. This reflects Kelly's own scientific and empirical orientation. Kelly's primary goal in the formulation of his theory was to reduce the amount of observer bias in the clinical setting and develop a measurement technique that allowed for assessment and understanding of an individual's perception of the world. That measurement technique is the extensively used Role Construct Repertory (REP) test.

Although Kelly's theory is more widely accepted and researched in Great Britain than in the United States, his work has had important applicability to a variety of fields across cultures, including psychotherapy, education, management, and artificial intelligence. In the business setting, for example, industrial psychologists and human resource managers use the REP test to interview employees and applicants. REP grid tests can be used to assess many characteristics, including dependency, flexibility, and decision-making. Kelly's theory and writings have also been influential in persuading psychologists to take a more empirical approach to understanding personality and to the therapy process.

Case Study 23
George Kelly

Maria, a marketing consultant, and Carlos, a computer programmer, have recently been blessed with their third child. They are in their late 20s and of Latino descent. After an uneventful pregnancy, Maria gave birth through a scheduled C-section to an 8 lb., 4 oz., healthy baby girl. The C-section was scheduled after Maria had had two unscheduled C-sections with her other children. In both cases, Maria had gone through labor, dilated fully, and pushed for an extended period, but unfortunately both babies were "stuck" and emergency C-sections were performed. Maria thought long and hard about whether she should try to give birth vaginally this time or whether she should just schedule the C-section. In making this decision, Maria did a lot of research and reading. There were pros and cons for both options. On the positive side: she would not have to go through labor, and she would know exactly when the baby was coming instead of waiting expectantly. On the negative side: she also knew that many C-sections are not necessary, that because it is major surgery there are increased risks, and that recovery from a C-section is usually harder than from a vaginal birth. Finally, in consultation with her doctor, she decided to schedule the caesarean. The whole procedure went well, and now, as she thinks back reassessing her decision, she feels it was a good one.

Being a parent and spouse are two very important sources of identity for both Carlos and Maria. Maria and Carlos agreed about having a family even before they got married; in their pre-engagement discussions, they found that for both of them, being married and having children was a priority in life. Further, in these discussions, Maria and Carlos found out that their ideas about how to parent were quite similar, although there were also some differences. For example, both thought that being a parent would be fun and that playing with their children was just as important as caring for their physical needs, but Carlos thought that Maria should give up her job and stay home with the kids full time. Maria thought working part-time and putting the kids in day care about 20 hours a week would be good. They also differed on more minor issues such as whether the children should open Christmas presents on Christmas Eve or Christmas Day and whether grandparents should do extensive amounts of baby-sitting. Both also understood that parenting was a lot of work and that they would feel tired occasionally. One thing that neither Carlos nor Maria understood, however, was just *how* much work parenting was and just *how* tired they would be all the time. They also did not count on having to give up activities that they enjoyed. When they had their first child, they continued to try to go out to nice restaurants and museums. They quickly found out how difficult those activities were with a child. So, Carlos and Maria changed their ideas about what parenting was: it wasn't just doing more because of the child; it was also doing less because of the child. Maria was also amazed to find out that being a mother meant being creative. She was continuously trying to come up with ways to get the children to do what she wanted them to do. Just telling them was not enough. Sometimes they would do just the opposite of what she wanted because they were trying to assert their independence. Initially, Maria dealt with these episodes of stubbornness by losing her temper. Even though she tried to be patient and wanted to be understanding, some days she could no longer stand the strain of being a mother and ended up snapping at the kids. After a while, she found that by making things into games, she could get her kids to cooperate more. By using this strategy, she lost her temper less frequently, but she understood that punishing a child or yelling at a child was also part of being a good parent. Children need to learn boundaries.

No doubt Carlos and Maria's ideas about parenting will continue to change with the growth of their newest family addition, but they now understand that good parenting means many changes.

APPLICATION QUESTIONS

Using Kelly's personal construct theory, analyze Maria and Carlos's behavior by answering the following questions.

1. Explain how Kelly's theory could suggest that Maria is a scientist.
2. What seems to be one of Maria and Carlos's important personal constructs? Explain the construct.
3. What did Kelly mean by the dichotomy corollary? Find an example of it in the case study.
4. What did Kelly mean by the individuality corollary? Find an example of it in the case study.
5. What did Kelly mean by the fragmentation corollary? Find an example of it in the case study.

6. What did Kelly mean by the commonality corollary? Find an example of it in the case study.

7. What does Kelly mean by a permeable construct? What does the experience corollary mean? What does the modulation corollary mean? Are Carlos and Maria's constructs permeable? Give examples of the experience and modulation corollaries.

THEORY COMPARISON QUESTIONS

1. Compare Kelly's concept of a construct to a schema.

2. Explain Maria's change in parenting style (e.g., her encouraging her children's cooperation by making requests into games after her requests were refused) using Bandura's concept of reciprocal determinism. How does Bandura's concept of reciprocal determinism compare with Kelly's theoretical concepts?

3. How could Skinner's radical behaviorism explain Maria's change in parenting style to encourage cooperation by her children? How does the focus of Skinner's theory differ from that of Kelly's theory?

Case Study 24

George Kelly

Philip is a member of the clergy, a priest in the Roman Catholic Church, and has been for almost 25 years. His religion has been important to him ever since he was a young child. He grew up in an Irish Catholic family that was involved in their parish and said grace before each meal. They went to church every Sunday, and Philip was an altar boy. It seemed natural for him to become a priest: He was involved in his church, had a strong faith, and had an uncle who was a priest, and a cousin who was a nun. His family looked highly on that occupation, and it seemed to be one of the most prestigious careers he could aspire to.

As he nears the 25th anniversary of his ordination into the priesthood, he reflects on the differences between members of the clergy and those who were not members of the clergy. He considers that clergy members have an incredibly important responsibility in guiding their followers spiritually. This responsibility weighs on him. Occasionally, he is envious of his parishioners who do not have this duty, but then he remembers how fortunate he is to be one of those God called to be a religious leader. It helps to discuss this concern with other clergy members who understand and experience this feeling of obligation as well. He also considers the things he has had to give up as a Roman Catholic priest. Priests are not allowed to marry and, indeed, even take a vow of chastity. It has been difficult for him to have never known the love of a woman and to never have children of his own. Likewise, not having had sex was difficult, especially when he was younger. It was more difficult to keep his vow of chastity than it was to keep his vow of obedience to the bishop. Now that he is getting older, that is not as much a concern. He comforts himself with the thoughts of the close friendships he has formed, the children of friends he has been able to enjoy, and the knowledge that he is doing God's will.

Leaders of other religious groups, however, do not believe that being a clergy member means giving up family life or sex. These clergy members are not required to take the vows of chastity that Philip did. Philip is aware of these differences and still believes that his requirements are the best way to serve God. Philip is also aware of a number of differences in the clergy within the Roman Catholic religion. In recent years, a number of priests and nuns have voiced opinions about changes that they believe should be made within the church. An example of this is the notion that the Catholic Church should allow women to become priests. Only men have been allowed to join the priesthood because of the accepted view that all 12 of Jesus Christ's apostles were men and the belief that the priest is the presence of Christ among the people, whom only a man can represent. Today, these reformers believe that women should also be allowed to become priests because of theological arguments and evidence that supports the idea that some of Jesus' disciples were female and because of the women's movement. For example, some feminist theological research suggests that women were early missionaries and apostles. Reformers believe that changes like these will modernize the church by relying on earlier church traditions and encourage people to come back to the Roman Catholic religion. Philip disagrees with them. He is not a reformer and does not understand the reasoning of these people. How could these church leaders revoke what they had been taught and what they swore to execute?

Philip also considers other difficulties he has encountered in his religious career. One of the most disconcerting experiences he has had to adjust to was how people reacted to him when they learned that he was a priest. Either people avoided him when they saw his collar, or, if they interacted with him, they were cautious about what they said. They were careful not to swear or say things that they thought would offend him. They were not themselves. He was aware of the change in people's behavior that he evoked. This made forming relationships outside the religious order difficult, and it made him uncomfortable.

Sometimes he would be invited over to a parishioner's house for dinner. He would enjoy talking to the smaller children who would ask questions like: "Do you wear your collar when you go swimming?" He found that talking to the children and answering their questions at their level would often put him more at ease with the parents. Philip liked to be able to take breaks from being a "holy man" and occasionally feel like one of a family.

APPLICATION QUESTIONS

Using Kelly's personal construct theory, analyze Philip's behavior by answering the following questions.

1. What is the organization of Philip's construct of clergy?

2. What are the two poles of Philip's clergy construct? What corollary does this apply to?

3. How is Philip's clergy construct the same as other peoples'? What corollary does this apply to?

4. How is Philip's clergy construct different than other peoples'? What corollary does this apply to?

5. Does Philip's clergy construct appear to be permeable? Why or why not?

6. What is the sociality corollary? Find an example of it in the case study.

THEORY COMPARISON QUESTIONS

1. How does Kelly's individuality corollary compare with Adler's concept of subjective perceptions?

2. Use Bandura's concept of self-regulation to explain Philip's maintaining his traditional religious beliefs, even when presented with reformist views. How does Bandura's concept of self-regulation compare with Kelly's modulation corollary?

Helpful Hints

Are you having a problem answering some of the application questions for Case 23 or 24? See if the following will help you.

You might find Kelly's theory a bit confusing but that's probably only because you are unfamiliar with the terms that he uses. Try to think of a personal construct as something similar to a schema. It is a hypothetical, cognitive structure that helps to organize and process information. These constructs follow a number of rules called corollaries. The wording of the corollaries is somewhat complex so let me simplify some of them. The individuality corollary basically means that if two people have the same construct, their ideas of what that construct *is* will vary.

Conversely, the commonality corollary suggests that when different people have the same construct, the constructs are sometimes similar in nature. Thus, there can be some overlap between constructs in individuals but they probably will not be identical. The fragmentation corollary suggests that even though we appear to act in ways that seem inconsistent, they are probably consistent under a *superordinate construct* (a construct near the top of the construct hierarchy). The experience corollary suggests that we change our constructs as we encounter experiences that do not fit our constructs. The modulation corollary means the more permeable a construct is, the more likely it is to change. (A permeable construct is one that *can* change.)

Burrhus Frederic Skinner
(1904–1990)

Radical Behaviorism
Why learn this theory?

Contributions

Skinner had a tremendous impact on the field of psychology, similar to the way Freud influenced the field earlier. Skinner's work helped the field of psychology to develop into a science. At a time when psychology was focused on internal, unmeasurable influences on behavior, Skinner rejected the idea of internal causes and, instead, began to study only measurable influences on behavior. He wanted to understand voluntary behavior in scientific terms. He wanted to understand how behavior is learned and then maintained.

Skinner is known as the Father of Radical Behaviorism. He developed the concept of operant conditioning (as opposed to Pavlov's classical conditioning that focused on involuntary behavior). Thus, he developed such useful concepts as reinforcement, schedules of reinforcement, and shaping. The operant conditioning approach developed into important strategies, especially in education. For example, the idea that teaching should consist of introducing material in consecutive stages developed from Skinner's notion of shaping (or successive approximation). The idea that student's behavior could be improved or controlled by the teacher through appropriate use of rewards and punishments also developed from Skinner's theory. The operant conditioning approach was also instrumental in the development of a variety of therapeutic practices. It was the building block of behavior modification, a therapy technique that extinguishes unwanted behavior and encourages desirable behavior, and the token economy, another behavior therapy technique that shapes behavior and is widely used in such settings as juvenile detention centers, psychiatric hospitals, and prisons. In fact, similar therapeutic techniques are widely used even by the general public. Parents use these behavioral techniques to encourage good behavior in their children and to discourage bad behavior. Dog trainers use these techniques so that our pets are well behaved. In sum, Skinner's theory transformed the field of psychology and encouraged a large number of practical applications in the areas of education, parenting, and therapy.

Case Study 25
Burrhus Frederic Skinner

Yolanda had always been an excellent student. In grade school, she always earned As and Bs, and the teachers always spoke highly of her during parent–teacher conferences. When her parents came home from these conferences, they often would repeat to her the positive remarks they had heard. She also excelled academically in high school even when she took advanced courses. She took algebra when she was in the eighth grade, college algebra as a junior, and calculus as a senior. She also took physics and advanced biology in the later part of high school. She was on the honor roll each semester, achieving a higher than 90 percent average each time. Again, teachers commented positively about her. The positive remarks and superior grades made her feel good about herself and boosted her self-esteem. At her high school graduation, she was valedictorian.

Understandably, Yolanda was college bound. She majored in psychology and again showed outstanding academic aptitude. Initially, Yolanda worked hard and earned excellent grades, but she was attending a large state university and the personal attention she was used to getting for her superior academic performance was not as readily forthcoming as it had been in grade school or high school. She no longer received trophies or certificates for doing well in her classes and, because most of her courses took place in large lecture halls that she attended with about 300 other students, her professors did not know who she was, let alone that she was one of the top students in the class. By her second semester, Yolanda's grades began to falter, and her GPA for the second semester turned out to be 2.01, a drop from her first-semester GPA of 3.5. By the end of her third semester, Yolanda was on probation. She decided to drop out of college and try working in the "real world" for a while.

Yolanda waited on tables for the next year and took stock of her life. She did not really enjoy her job. She did not make as much money as she would have liked and was tired of rude and inconsiderate customers. She felt as though she could do more, and she felt embarrassed when she told old friends from high school that she was no longer attending college. She felt as though they were looking down on her. She also felt as though she had disappointed her parents. They had encouraged Yolanda to achieve, partly for her benefit but, because of discrimination they had faced during the 1960s and 1970s, partly to demonstrate to the world that African Americans could achieve as much as others. She then decided to try college again.

She applied to a smaller college close to home and was pleased to find that she was not a number there but rather a person to whom professors talked. She majored again in psychology, got to know her professors, and studied hard. She did well in her courses, achieving a 3.6 GPA her first semester back in school. She soon became known within the psychology department as a rising star. Her professors talked to her, listened to her ideas and questions, and guided her toward graduate school. Her advisor suggested that she conduct some research if she was interested in attending graduate school because competition for graduate studies in psychology is fierce. She would need to stand out from other good students to be accepted into a program. She began a research project the second semester of her junior year and completed it the first semester of her senior year. Under the guidance of her research advisor, she submitted her research findings to the Eastern Psychological Association, and it was accepted as a poster presentation.

Yolanda's superior college grades (she ended up with a 3.8 GPA), her good Graduate Record Exam scores, and her research presentation helped her gain admission into a clinical psychology graduate program at a prestigious university. There, she worked closely with a number of advisors and eventually earned her Ph.D. She now works as a psychology professor at a small undergraduate college.

APPLICATION QUESTIONS

Using Skinner's radical behaviorism theory, analyze Yolanda's behavior by answering the following questions.

1. What motivates our behavior, according to Skinner's theory? Is it internally or externally motivated?

2. How could Yolanda's early success in school be explained by radical behaviorism?

3. How could radical behaviorism explain Yolanda's dropping out of college?

4. How could Skinner's theory explain Yolanda's decision to go back to college?

5. How could Skinner's theory explain Yolanda's success in college the second time and in graduate school?

THEORY COMPARISON QUESTIONS

1. Use another theory, besides Skinner's, to explain Yolanda's academic success.

2. How could Adler's individual personality theory explain Yolanda's success? How does the focus of Adler's theory differ from that of Skinner's?

3. Use Bandura's concept of self-regulation to explain Yolanda's progression through her career.

Case Study 26
Burrhus Frederic Skinner

It is Saturday night, and Colleen is sitting in her dorm room alone, working on her nails, listening to music, and wondering what is happening to her. She is an 18-year-old college freshman from Mississippi attending a university in the Northeast and is having some trouble adjusting to college life. It seems to her as though people "up North" value completely different behavior than the people she grew up with in the South, and she is no longer as popular and as respected as she was back home. She is confused and depressed.

Colleen grew up in a family with a strong Southern heritage. Both her mother and her father were born in Mississippi, and their ancestors could be traced back to the Civil War. In fact, both families could boast that their ancestors had actually fought in the Civil War. This heritage was instilled in Colleen, who was also proud to be a Southerner and to have such a distinguished ancestry. As a child, Colleen would hear the stories of her relatives' past not only from her parents, but also from her grandparents. She could tell that they were proud of their lineage, and they were always pleased when someone expressed interest in their stories. When Colleen showed such interest, they showed their pleasure with a smile or a hug and kiss. Sometimes they remarked what a good girl she was. As a teenager, Colleen was elected to the prestigious organization called the Daughters of the Confederacy, an organization in which she could socialize with influential others. To be elected to this organization, one had to be able to trace one's ancestors back to the Civil War.

Colleen always seemed to be very interested in social events. She often helped to organize them in high school, and it was crucial to her that the "right people" were at the "right parties" or "events." As a cheerleader, she organized events such as class rallies and bonfires, and she hosted her own pre-prom party. Colleen was always popular in high school because of these events. She was the person who knew everything about everyone, and others were always interested in finding out the latest gossip from her. Her mother let Colleen know how proud she was of Colleen's ability to organize these social events and about her popularity, unlike Colleen's older sister, Kaye. Their mother often hosted social events herself and prided herself on her own abilities as a hostess. Kaye, on the other hand, seemed to be just the opposite of her mother and younger sister. She was not interested in organizing social events and didn't seem to care about becoming a member of the Daughters of the Confederacy—she actually de-emphasized her heritage. For example, whereas Kaye worked hard to de-emphasize her Southern accent, Colleen emphasized hers such that she actually had a stronger accent than either of her parents. Whereas Colleen was very interested in clothes and makeup, Kaye was not interested in them at all and often looked more masculine, even in body type. Colleen was very slight and avoided physical activity other than her cheer-leading; Kaye had a more athletic build and was on the track team.

Both sisters were smart: But whereas Kaye had no problems with others knowing she did well in school, Colleen preferred to not let on that she did well and would sometimes pretend to not know something when she did know. She rarely spoke up in class and was often referred to as a perfect student by her teachers. Kaye, on the other hand, was very vocal and sometimes challenged her teachers. Their mother preferred Colleen to Kaye because Colleen was more similar to their mother. Kaye knew that her mother disapproved of her behavior but did not care.

Now it seems to Colleen that everyone at college, except her, is more like her sister than like her mother. The other students have remarked about Colleen's Southern accent and have suggested she try to tame it because it makes her sound stupid. The other students have not enjoyed her gossiping because they believe she is betraying confidences. Even the way she dresses does not fit in with the other students. She wears dresses or designer jeans and makeup all the time; her roommates wear jeans and tee shirts and no makeup. Some of the other women even have their noses pierced and tattoos on their bodies. Colleen's grades are hurting too. Many of her professors require class participation; students' grades are partly determined by that, but Colleen is reluctant to talk in class, thinking that it seems like showing off. Her fellow students, who value intelligence, are beginning to wonder if Colleen is stupid because she is still hiding what she knows.

Colleen wishes she had never left the South. She had followed her boyfriend to college, in the North, and now he has left her for another woman he met in one of his classes only four weeks into the semester! Now she has no female friends and even the men in her classes are not interested in her. At home, boys continually asked her out; now the men she is interested in are not interested in her. She is wondering whether she should finish the semester or whether she should just go back home now and transfer to a Southern college.

APPLICATION QUESTIONS

Using Skinner's radical behaviorism theory, analyze Colleen's behavior by answering the following questions.

1. According to Skinner's theory, why did Colleen express so much interest in her heritage and in social events?

2. What reinforced Colleen's interests in her heritage and in social events, according to Skinner's theory? Give specific examples. Are they primary or secondary reinforcers? Explain.

3. Which of Colleen's behaviors are not rewarded in college anymore? What term in radical behaviorism could be used to describe this?

4. According to radical behaviorism, why would Colleen be experiencing depression?

5. According to Skinner's theory, why would Colleen transfer out of college?

THEORY COMPARISON QUESTIONS

1. How does Bandura's concept of reinforcement compare with Skinner's?

2. Apply Kelly's personal construct theory to Colleen's college experiences. What appear to be her superordinate constructs? Are her constructs permeable?

3. Use Erikson's crisis concepts of identity versus role confusion and intimacy versus isolation to explain Colleen's college experiences. How does the focus of Erikson's theory compare with that of Skinner's theory?

4. Use May's concepts of alienation and the human dilemma to explain Colleen's college experiences.

Helpful Hints

Are you having a problem answering some of the application questions for Case 25 or 26? See if the following will help you.

Skinner did not discuss the existence or influence of personality but if one had to develop a definition of personality in radical behaviorism, it would have to be the sum total of our conditioning history. In determining why certain behaviors occur or are avoided, focus on rewards and punishments. Remember that behaviors can be eliminated by withholding rewards (extinction) and that similar behaviors can occur, although they have not been individually rewarded because of generalization. Keep in mind that rewards do not have to be concrete. They may be intangible, and certain rewards may be reinforcing (or punishing) to some but not to others. Thus, a behavior may be reinforced for one person using one particular reward, but using that reward with another person might not result in the desired reinforcement.

Albert Bandura (1925–)

Social Cognitive Theory
Why learn this theory?

Contributions

Whereas Skinner suggested that behavior could only be learned by performing it, because it was only after its performance that reinforcement could occur, Bandura demonstrated that behavior could be learned even without performing it, thereby distinguishing between learning and performance. He was instrumental in demonstrating that cognitive factors were involved in learning, not just consequences of our behavior. In fact, he was one of the founders of the cognitive revolution in psychology during the 1960s; his model for self-regulation demonstrates the importance of cognitive factors on our behavior.

Bandura's theory is referred to as social learning theory, and certain aspects of the theory are referred to as observational learning or modeling or vicarious learning. His work on observational learning is some of his most well known and has been especially influential in the development of research on the effects of media violence on children's aggressive behavior. It has also seen practical applications such as in the development of modeling therapy that has been shown to be especially effective in treating phobias, like that of snakes. Likewise, the concept of observational learning has influenced the educational system, as well as parenting style. Because of it, teachers and parents now understand that they must model the behavior

that they desire in children. The "Do as I say, not as I do" command is no longer an appropriate mandate from either parents or teachers.

Like Skinner, Bandura's theory can be seen as a learning theory. However, Bandura's theory also contributes tremendously to the field of personality. In particular, Bandura's triadic reciprocal determinism model encourages personality theorists to consider the interaction between personality factors and the environment on influencing behavior, rather than considering the influence of personality singularly. The reciprocal determinism model suggests that person factors, behavior, and the environment all influence each other. Personality can be seen as one of the many person factors in Bandura's model. Consequently, Bandura's concept of self-efficacy can be seen as a person factor. Self-efficacy, too, is an especially relevant concept for education and parenting. Both parents and teachers must be able to develop efficacy in children in order to help them learn. Thus, building confidence and setting up realistic expectations that children can meet are vitally important in a well-run classroom and in family situations. In sum, Bandura's theory has influenced the therapeutic practices of psychologists, the educational practices of teachers, and the child-rearing practices of parents.

Case Study 27
Albert Bandura

Drew has returned to Albany, New York, for the memorial service of his dear friend Ruth. He lived with Ruth for three years while he was attending school in Albany. He was 23 at the time he moved in; Ruth was 73. His cousin, who attended the same church as Ruth, introduced the two of them because Ruth occasionally rented out two of her rooms to boarders. As a close friend of Ruth's, Drew is to deliver a eulogy in her honor. As he sits down to write his tribute, he contemplates Ruth's remarkable life.

Ruth, the third child in a family with six children, lost her sight when she was just five years old. At a time before antibiotics were developed, she had contracted meningitis and had to stay in bed for a week with a high fever. The doctor did not think she would survive. She did survive; unfortunately, however, she lost her sight. She was determined, though, to live her life as a "normal" child—that is, one who could see. This determination was sometimes taken too far, and Drew still smiles as he recalls some of the stories Ruth told about her childhood. She would roller-skate with her friends and even learned to ride a bike! On at least one occasion, Ruth walked on top of a fence—without assistance! A neighbor stopped her before she got to the end of the fence and fell off. Ruth wanted to go to school like her brothers and sisters but at that time, visually impaired children did not attend public school. Ruth made her brothers and sisters do their homework aloud so she could learn.

Ruth expressed feeling sorry for herself only once. She was frustrated with her inability to do something that seeing people could do easily. When she expressed her frustration, her mother started to cry. Noticing how upset her mother was about Ruth's distress, Ruth never again expressed sorrow at her loss of sight.

When Ruth was 10 or 11, she took the train from Jamestown to Batavia to attend the Batavia School for the Blind. There she learned survival skills, including Braille, typing, and ways that visually impaired people could get along in a world full of people with sight. For example, she learned to put a piece of tape under the salt shaker so that it could be distinguished from the pepper shaker; she learned to distinguish between dollar bills of varying amounts by putting paper clips on them.

As an adult, Ruth continued to be very independent. She could have had a guide dog when they began to be used, but felt that they limited her independence because they had to be cared for. She had a white cane, but did not want to use it, thinking the cane made her condition too obvious. And Ruth did not want to be obvious. In fact, she was determined to behave in the same ways seeing people did. She sometimes did such a good job at it that others thought she could see. Once, when she was at the dentist's, he held out an instrument for her to take; Ruth, of course, could not see it and so did not take it. He asked her why she wouldn't take the instrument and was surprised when she replied that she did not see. He had had no idea about her visual impairment. Ruth was quite proud of that story. More than anything, she did not want to stand out from others, especially from those who could see.

Ruth felt that visually impaired people were discriminated against in society and were sometimes perceived as a burden. They were also sometimes viewed as having other disabilities besides blindness. For example, strangers would sometimes talk loudly to her even though there was nothing wrong with her hearing. When she was out at a restaurant with someone, the server would sometimes ask her friend what Ruth wanted to eat, as though she was mentally incapacitated as well. So, Ruth did her best to behave as seeing people did.

As an adult, Ruth was a home teacher for the blind until she met Kevin, who became her husband. They met at a social function for visually impaired people; Kevin was also visually impaired, although not totally blind like Ruth. After they were married, Ruth helped her husband manage his newspaper/candy stand, which was located in a factory in Buffalo. This was a state job geared specifically for the visually impaired, and they sold assorted sundries. Later they moved to Albany and managed a similar stand at the state capital. This was a very interesting enterprise because Kevin and Ruth were able to meet and get to know many politicians. They knew all the assemblymen and all the governors, and, likewise, the politicians knew them. Ruth's favorite governor was Nelson Rockefeller. She thought he was very energetic.

Kevin and Ruth retired after a number of years and, as is fairly typical, her husband preceded Ruth in death. She lived alone for a number of years until some friends encouraged her to help Drew by taking him in as a boarder. Ruth initially did not want Drew as a boarder. It had been years since she had had a boarder, and she wasn't sure she wanted to adjust to a new one. Conversely, it was Drew who had some trouble adjusting to living with Ruth. Her house was always neat as a pin, and she always had a place for everything. She had to. Because she could not see, she had to keep things where they belonged so that she could find them, and she had to keep the house clean so that she would not trip and fall on something that was left out. Drew was fairly disorganized and sloppy. Eventually he adjusted to Ruth's lifestyle, and they became good friends. Drew thought that one of the reasons why Ruth's mind remained so sharp, even until her death, was the fact that she continuously used it to compensate for her not being able to rely on her sight. Eventually, Drew married and moved away, but Ruth and he kept in touch with phone calls. In many ways, Ruth was a surrogate mother to Drew, and he knew he would certainly miss her.

APPLICATION QUESTIONS

Using Bandura's social cognitive theory, explain Ruth's personality by answering the following questions.

1. What does Bandura mean by reciprocal determinism? Find an example of it in the case and describe the interrelationships between the factors.

2. What does Bandura mean by self-regulation? Find an example of it in the case and describe it. Be sure to mention each of the stages of self-regulation involved in the example; that is, what happens during the self-monitoring, self-evaluation, and self-reaction stages?

3. What are some external factors involved in self-regulation? Explain them through the use of your self-regulation example.

THEORY COMPARISON QUESTIONS

1. What fortuitous event had a major impact on Ruth's life? What does Bandura's theory say about such events? How does this aspect of his theory differ from other personality theories?

2. Apply Adler's theory to Ruth's life. Specifically, discuss her striving for success and style of life. Compare Adler's theory with Bandura's.

3. Apply Erikson's theory to Ruth's life. Which stages appear to have been completed successfully? Which have not? Explain. Compare Erikson's theory to Bandura's.

Case Study 28
Albert Bandura

E vonne is sitting at the table with a cup of tea. She has just tucked her kids into bed, and this is the first time she has had to herself all day. She wonders if her decision to stay at home was the right one. Her days as a mother and homemaker are certainly more exhausting than were those when she worked as a bookkeeper at a physician's office. She is continuously cleaning the house or meeting the demands of her children. It is amazing how much mess such little people can make. It seems as though they drop what they have in their hands anywhere they stand. Her son, Joe, for example, comes in from school, takes off his coat, and drops it, along with his backpack, on the kitchen floor in front of the door through which he came in. He places his hat and mittens on the kitchen cupboard located next to the door he just walked through. Sometimes, when he is excited to show his mother something he made at school, Joe dumps his backpack out onto the floor to find it. When he is through, he leaves the rest of the stuff on the floor and runs off to play with his sister. Although Evonne keeps reminding Joe to pick up his things and put them where they belong, he does not seem to remember to do it from one day to the next. Not surprisingly, Joe often cannot find the things he needs because he did not put them in their place when he was through with them. In that way he is a lot like his father, Blake, who is always losing and looking for things, especially his wallet, because he does not put his belongings in the right place either. Now that Evonne thought about it, Blake seemed to drop things wherever he was standing also, and although Evonne scolded Joe for it, she rarely complained to Blake about his sloppiness—at least not in front of the children.

As Evonne thought about how Joe resembled Blake in this regard, she also noticed other similarities in their behavior. Lately, Joe has been trying to deflect punishment for wrongdoing by charming his way out of it. It struck Evonne that this was similar to Blake's behavior when he made her angry: he would often try to alleviate the mood and avoid an argument by complimenting her or joking about his or her behavior that they were discussing. Sometimes it worked, and she laughed, hugged, and kissed her husband; sometimes it didn't work. Now Joe was doing the same thing. When he said something to her that he shouldn't have, for example, Joe would laugh and give her a big smile and bat his eyelashes at her. Sometimes she couldn't help but laugh back.

At other times, Joe would just try to make his mother laugh by telling jokes. He loved to see her smile. Most of the time, his jokes were pretty bad, but every once in a while he would tell a good one, and Evonne would chuckle. Recently, Joe has been asking whether his jokes were good or not. He is disappointed when his mother tells him that his joke is not one of his best and thrilled when she says it is good.

Joe does other things that his father does as well. For example, Joe calls out "special night!" when he wants to just have fun that evening and watch a video and eat popcorn. Blake would sometimes call out that phrase or something similar when he wanted to have fun with his family and when there would be no work that day. Joe even wants a "libation"—a fun drink such as a soda—on these occasions, and Evonne knows that Joe picked up that term from Blake, who also enjoys grown-up "libations." Joe, for example, drinks root beer when his father has a beer.

Joe seems to have his father's self-confidence also. For example, Joe, at the age of eight, is a little computer whiz. He saw his father working on their home computer and his peers working on the computers at day care when he was younger. He had had no qualms about sitting down at the monitor and trying to play various games. He became frustrated at times, but Blake encouraged him. Joe eventually learned how to use the mouse and became quite proficient at computerized tasks. This amazed Evonne because, although she now knows how to use the computer, she at first was terribly intimidated by computers and thought that she would never be able to understand them. Joe has had no such reservations. Yes, there really were quite a few similarities between Joe and Blake. The phrase "like father, like son" comes to Evonne's mind.

APPLICATION QUESTIONS

Using Bandura's social cognitive theory, explain the similarities between Joe and Blake's personalities by answering the following questions.

1. How could Bandura's social cognitive theory explain the similarity between Joe and Blake's behaviors?

2. List some examples of observational learning from the case.

3. What factors determine whether or not we will learn from a model, according to Bandura's theory? Choose one example of behavior learned through modeling from the case and explain the influence of these factors.

4. Find an example of self-regulation that Joe engages in. Explain it.

5. How could Bandura's theory explain Joe's confidence in using computers and his competence in using them?

THEORY COMPARISON QUESTIONS

1. Use Skinner's radical behaviorism to explain Joe's computer competence. How does Skinner's explanation compare with Bandura's explanation?

2. What behavioral techniques could Evonne use to encourage Blake and Joe to become neater? Explain.

3. Apply Kelly's personal construct theory to Blake and Joe's behaviors. Specifically, use the sociality corollary to explain Joe manipulating his mother (by giving her cute looks) to avoid punishment; use the commonality corollary to explain Joe and Blake's sloppiness. Compare Kelly's experience corollary with Bandura's concept of modeling.

Helpful Hints

Are you having a problem with answering some of the application questions for Case 27 or 28? See if the following will help you.

Remember that Bandura's concept of self-efficacy is fairly specific. It is *not* a general form of confidence. Rather, self-efficacy is a belief that we either can or cannot execute a *certain* behavior. When our self-efficacy is high, we believe that we can perform the behavior, and this belief makes it more likely that we can perform it successfully. When our self-efficacy is low, we have little confidence that we can perform the behavior successfully and we are actually less likely to do so. Self-efficacy can be thought of as a P (person) factor in Bandura's reciprocal determinism model whereby person (P) factors (such as thoughts), the environment (E) (such as rewards and punishments), and behavior (B) all influence each other in any given situation. Remember also that self-efficacy is *not* a belief about what will happen if we perform a certain behavior, that is, consequences or rewards and punishments (E factors); it is just the belief that we can or cannot perform it.

Julian Rotter (1916–)

Social Learning Theory
Why learn this theory?

Contributions

Julian Rotter's most notable contributions to personality psychology include his social learning theory and his concept of locus of control. In his social learning theory, Rotter emphasized the influence of cognitive and environmental factors, in addition to psychological factors, on behavior. He suggested that our expectancies were important in determining our behaviors. For example, if we think that a positive experience is likely when we engage in a behavior, then there is an increased chance of us engaging in that particular behavior than if we believe that the behavior will have a negative outcome. Rotter recognized that humans are cognitive beings influenced by the environment, as well as other psychological factors. In fact, Rotter's emphasis on cognitive factors can be seen as instrumental in the development of cognitive-behavioral therapies.

Rotter's locus of control is also of great significance to the field of personality psychology. Rotter suggested that some people feel as though they have more control over their circumstances than do others. Those who feel as though they have control are said to have an internal locus of control. Those who feel as though they lack control over their environment are said to have an external locus of control. This concept has had significant applicability in the therapy field and in health psychology. Research has demonstrated, for example, that people with an external locus of control are more prone to depression. And those with an external health locus of control may be less likely to engage in healthy habits that can prevent illness. Rotter's I-E scale, which measures internal and external locus of control, is widely used in the field of personality psychology, and this concept has generated a great deal of research.

Case Study 29
Julian Rotter

I t is late March, and Barb is thinking back on New Year's Eve and her New Year's resolution. She, like millions of others, wanted to "get healthy." In other words she wanted to eat better, exercise more, and lose some weight. Her ultimate weight loss goal was 40 pounds but she said she would be happy with losing about 25. This was actually a goal for her for a number of years—ever since she put on weight during her pregnancies. Barb had gained more weight during her two pregnancies than was recommended and, after childbirth, she did not have the time or energy to take it off. But now her children are growing up and need less attention. Likewise, Barb has an added incentive: just after Thanksgiving, her sister, Lisa, who is only five years older than her, had a stroke. Lisa survived the stroke but experienced some paralysis that required physical therapy. Although she has been able to regain much of the use of her right arm, her speech is still a little slurred. The stroke was due to her sister's high blood pressure, of which she was unaware. Like Barb, Lisa was over-weight and did not exercise, conditions that can increase the risk of high blood pressure and the subsequent risk of stroke and heart disease.

After her sister's health scare, Barb decided to get a physical and discuss a weight loss program with her physician. She found out that she did not have high blood pressure, but was borderline for the condition. Her physician did state that exercise and some weight loss should reduce her blood pressure. Since then Barb started walking regularly and has cut back on eating junk food. Initially, weight loss was slow but the first three pounds she lost motivated her enough to stay with her plan. She's been able to lose 12 pounds and her friends are starting to comment about her looking good. Barb enjoys this attention. Before she was married and had children, she was fairly slender, not as thin as is fashionable today, but well within a normal weight range, and she enjoyed the way she looked back then. She's beginning to feel better about the way she looks now and wants to feel sexy and attractive as she did when she was younger. One of the things she learned from her mother when she was growing up was that people respond positively if a woman is attractive. Thus, her mother had always harped on dressing well, wearing makeup, fixing her hair, and watching what she ate so that she would not become too heavy. At the same time though, whenever Barb or Lisa were upset about something, her mother tried to comfort them by offering them treats like homemade cookies. When Barb had gained weight during the process of having children, her mother commented about "letting herself go" and said that Barb needed to be careful her husband didn't look at other women. Barb wasn't worried about her husband having affairs; they had a healthy relationship. But she had developed a love/hate relationship with food that resulted in poor eating habits and weight gain.

Barb went to a nutritionist after the first of the year to discuss her eating habits and develop a diet plan. During the discussion, Barb realized that she really likes to cook and eat good food but often the way she prepared it resulted in too many calories. Barb also discussed with the nutritionist *when* she ate badly. She came to realize that she used food as comfort in times of stress. For example, when she had a stressful time with her kids or a tough time at work, Barb looked forward to taking a break by having a dessert and a cup of coffee to relax; however, these "comfort sessions" were occurring too often. The nutritionist suggested substitutions for some of Barb's favorite recipes and other ways of reducing stress besides eating (e.g., taking a walk or some other type of exercise; a hot bath; going out with friends). Overeating at parties, picnics, and other social gatherings was also problematic. But the nutritionist pointed out that lapses in good eating habits were acceptable, as long as they didn't happen as often as they had been for Barb. People can actually take a short break from dieting and still lose weight. Relatedly, and conversely, because there are so many occasions that call for social eating, Barb shouldn't feel as though she *had* to choose high-calorie foods at parties because she doesn't get them often. The fact is that she probably did get to eat them often, but didn't notice. It seems as though every month there is something to celebrate: Thanksgiving, Christmas, New Year's, Valentine's Day, and so on, so treats are readily available but should not be included in one's daily diet. Finally, Barb also noticed during their discussions that she tends to eat when she is watching television, and the nutritionist suggested that she purchase a treadmill and watch television only when she is walking on the treadmill.

Barb is feeling much better than she did before the holidays. She feels more attractive and has more energy. Occasionally, she returns to her old eating habits, but not often. She recalls feeling guilty and disgusted after eating junk food before her lifestyle change and doesn't want to feel that way again. She hopes to lose five more pounds before summer so she can feel good about wearing a bathing suit again.

APPLICATION QUESTIONS

Using Rotter's social learning theory, analyze Barb's behavior by answering the following questions.

1. What is minimal goal level, according to Rotter? Find an example of it in the case study.
2. What type of locus of control does Barb appear to have? Provide evidence for your answer.
3. Use Rotter's concept of reinforcement value to explain Barb's choosing between healthy lower calorie food and higher calorie comfort food (e.g., junk food).
4. Use Rotter's psychological needs and his concept of freedom of movement to explain Barb's need to lose weight and feel attractive again.
5. Use Rotter's concept of expectancy to explain Barb's avoidance of eating junk food.
6. Use Rotter's concept of behavior potential and his views on situational factors to explain Barb's eating habits while watching television, when she is stressed, and at parties.

THEORY COMPARISON QUESTIONS

1. Compare Rotter's freedom of movement to Adler's feelings of inferiority.
2. How is Rotter's concept of locus of control similar to Bandura's concept of self-efficacy? How is it different?

Case Study 30
Julian Rotter

Randall is a 16-year-old about to begin serving a sentence in a juvenile detention center for building a bomb that he intended to use against his ex-girlfriend, Jenny. He and a friend had hoped to plant it in a place he knew Jenny and her friends hung out to get revenge for breaking up with him. But fortunately, although he had built the bomb, he did not get the chance to hide it or detonate it. By a quirk of fate, he and his mother had been evicted from the house they had been living in because they had not paid their rent for the last four months. They had returned home one evening and found a padlock on the door and a note explaining that they could not enter the premises until they had paid the rent owed. The bomb was located in Randall's room, where he had built it. Randall couldn't believe how unlucky he was: first he and his mother were kicked out of their home; then the landlord found the bomb and called the authorities.

It seemed as though these types of things always happened to him. He had the worst luck. At school it seemed as though the teachers were against him too. They put trick questions on exams so that he did poorly and made all kinds of unreasonable assignments that took too much time to complete. They didn't even remind you about when they were due, and he always lost points because he handed them in late. He felt that no matter how much he worked, he couldn't pull his grades up and that graduating from high school seemed a remote possibility. You couldn't trust teachers. They were always looking for ways to trick students.

Randall didn't think he could trust the other students either. He found out early that people generally couldn't be relied upon. He believes he should only rely on himself because others will just let you down. His father left him and his mother years ago, and his mother is an alcoholic who has never been very attentive. When she gets drunk, she gets verbally abusive. When this happens, Randall usually leaves their home and goes for a walk or to a friend's house to hang out.

Interestingly, although Randall endures his mother's verbal assaults, he does not put up with any other verbal insults in school or out of school. If someone makes a snide comment about him, Randall is immediately in that person's face, retaliating with verbal attacks and threatening physical harm until they back down or until a fight starts. Randall knows that he risks being expelled from school if he starts another fight but the attention and respect he gets by not taking any abuse from anyone and by being intimidating are more important to him. Even though he'd like to finish high school he thinks it unlikely that he will be able to do so, considering how many teachers dislike him and how poor his grades are. Now, with his imminent incarceration, it is even less likely. But, acquiring respect is more important than getting that piece of paper they call a high school diploma. Besides, getting a GED is just as good as a diploma with no work involved, or so Randall supposed.

APPLICATION QUESTIONS

Using Rotter's social learning theory, analyze Randall's behavior by answering the following questions.

1. What is locus of control, according to Rotter? What type of locus of control does Randall appear to have? Provide evidence for your answer.

2. How does Rotter describe interpersonal trust? Would Randall score high or low in interpersonal trust? Provide evidence for your answer.

3. What is behavior potential, according to Rotter? Find an example of it in the case study. What does Rotter say about the importance of the situation in determining behavior?

4. What is expectancy and reinforcement value, according to Rotter? How do they influence Randall's decision to argue/fight with a schoolmate who is verbally abusive?

5. What is freedom of movement, according to Rotter? Use Rotter's psychological needs and the concept of freedom of movement to explain Randall's decision to argue/fight with a schoolmate who is verbally abusive.

THEORY COMPARISON QUESTIONS

1. Use Horney's theory to explain Randall's behavior.

2. Use Skinner's radical behaviorism to explain Randall's aggressive behavior. Compare and contrast Rotter's thoughts on reinforcement to those of Skinner.

Helpful Hints

Are you having a problem with answering some of the application questions for Case 29 or 30? See if the following will help you.

Rotter is probably most known for his work on internal and external locus of control, but his theory consists of more than just that concept. In brief, his theory states that behavior is determined, not by just one variable, but rather by a number of factors. These include behavior potential, expectancy, reinforcement value, and the situation. Behavior potential is the likelihood of a behavior occurring in a certain situation. Expectancy refers to beliefs about the behavior or situation and what might happen if one behaves in a certain way in a certain situation. Reinforcement value refers to how rewarding a certain reinforcement is to a particular person. Finally, people behave differently in different situations. Thus, what Rotter suggested is that we determine our behavior by examining the situation, evaluating what might happen if we behave in a certain way in that situation, and choosing the most potentially rewarding course of action.

Although this aspect of Rotter's theory is fairly straightforward, students sometimes find his concept of freedom of movement a bit confusing. Freedom of movement is also an expectancy but it is more specific than the expectancy discussed above. It refers to an expectancy about whether a behavior will lead to the desired reward (success). Thus, we can have low or high freedom of movement depending on whether we believe our behavior will be successful (high freedom of movement) or not (low freedom of movement). Note that these expectancies are not always accurate.

Gordon Allport (1897–1967)

Trait Theory
Why learn this theory?

Contributions

Although Gordon Allport is considered a pioneer in personality psychology and sometimes referred to as founder of the field, he is also well known in the field of social psychology, strongly influencing that field with his writings on attitudes and on prejudice in particular. He is best known for his trait theory of personality that he developed by examining every term in a dictionary that could be considered a personality trait. After developing a list of thousands of possible traits, he categorized them according to their importance and pervasiveness. Thus, Allport developed a hierarchy, suggesting that there were three different types of traits: cardinal traits, which dominate a person's life but are rarely found; central traits, which are general and influence most of our behaviors; and secondary traits, which are situationally defined.

Allport's view of behavior was eclectic. He thought that behavior was both internally and externally motivated, thereby suggesting that certain aspects of both the psychodynamic and behavioral views had relevance in the understanding of behavior. He referred to these internal and external influences on behavior as genotypes and phenotypes, respectively. Similarly, Allport was known for his emphasis on the uniqueness of the individual. This, along with his concept of the proprium, a creative, growth-seeking motivation in humans, has a humanistic flavor.

Case Study 31
Gordon Allport

Monica is a 38-year-old stay-at-home mother of four children. She is starting to become a bit bored with staying home, having done that for the past 15 years. Prior to having children, she worked in a credit union and enjoyed that job. She especially liked the precision of the number crunching. This is a characteristic that she has carried into her housekeeping chores. She tries to keep her home spotless, even with four children. She cleans the two bathrooms everyday, vacuums, dusts, picks up toys, and so forth. Clutter and messiness bother her, and she is almost neurotic about cleaning. She's a perfectionist and knows it. All her friends agree, but she is able to laugh at this quirk and not take herself too seriously.

Although maintaining a house with four children might seem overwhelming to others, Monica handles these chores fine and has time (sometimes while she is cleaning) to keep in close touch with many friends, especially with phone calls. She is continuously on the phone. Her friends are a very important part of her social support network, especially since she does not have coworkers with whom to interact and because her husband travels a lot for his job. Often, her friends seem more important to her than her spouse, and she seems to have a better relationship with them than her husband. They describe her as being fiercely loyal, supportive, and talkative. They also know she has a good heart: She's always willing to help out another mom whose babysitter got sick by watching their child while she goes to work. Or if a friend is feeling overwhelmed about preparing for an upcoming party, she's willing to cook or bake something for them. You would never know from looking at her that Monica is such a warm and caring person. She actually looks a bit intimidating and angry but that's just because her age is starting to show with somewhat deep lines between her eyes being mistaken for frowning. She's aware of this contradiction and is a bit self-conscious of her frown lines.

She is also insecure about not having attended college. Many of her friends graduated from college; some even have master's degrees, but Monica never did. She doesn't think of herself as unintelligent, but sees herself as uneducated and defers to others with a better education. Her friends see her as very intelligent, and they encourage her to pursue at least an associate's degree, mainly so that she would feel better about herself. Monica is considering this possibility. It's something that she has always wanted to do. In particular, she is thinking about getting an associate's degree in Legal Business Studies and becoming a legal assistant after all her children are in middle school. They will be old enough to not need her as much, but that is still two years away, and she is nervous about this prospect because she has been out of school for so long.

Monica is a good mother. She takes care of her children's physical and emotional needs. She has one child, Jenna, who has a severe learning disability, and she is a consistent advocate for her. She makes sure that Jenna's needs are met, but she is realistic. She knows that Jenna will probably not go as far as her other three children in whatever her chosen career is. Monica is pragmatic that way, even though it is painful for her.

Monica also makes sure that her children have fun. Their family usually purchases a Six Flags Amusement Park season's pass, and they frequently go during the summers and even into the fall. At first she went on some of the more exciting roller coasters just because her children wanted to try them out but now she is an avid roller-coaster fan and would ride on them even if her children were not with her. This sense of fun can likewise be found in her ability to laugh at herself. She is able to see humor in her need for order and cleanliness, as mentioned earlier, and in her tendency to not be able to recall a word she wants to use (the notorious tip-of-the-tongue phenomenon) and her occasional feelings of frustration as she takes care of her children. She sometimes loses her temper, especially when she is tired, but she is always aware of her fatigue being a factor in how she reacts to her children. She can later joke about this with friends who also have children, and sometimes even with her own kids.

APPLICATION QUESTIONS

Using Allport's trait theory approach, describe Monica's personality by answering the following questions.

1. Allport suggested seven criteria that demonstrate that a person is psychologically healthy (mature). What are they? Find examples of them in the case.

2. What are the differences between cardinal, central, and secondary traits? What are some of Monica's central traits?

3. What is functional autonomy? Find an example of preservative functional autonomy in the case.

4. What is proprium, according to Allport? What is Monica's proprium?

5. What is propriate striving? Find an example of it in the case.

THEORY COMPARISON QUESTIONS

1. Compare Allport's criteria for mental health to those of other theorists.
2. How does Allport's propriate striving compare to Jung's concept of self-realization? To Maslow's concept of actualization? To Rogers' concept of actualization?
3. Compare Allport's concept of the proprium to Rogers' concept of the self.

Case Study 32
Gordon Allport

Grace is a 55-year-old Caucasian, widowed, with one grown daughter. Her husband died unexpectedly of a heart attack five years ago. Since then she has become an avid pro-life activist. She had never been involved in those types of activities before but after her husband's death she needed something to ease the pain and make life more meaningful. She was raised in the Roman Catholic faith so it was natural that she took solace in her religion. She finds comfort and security in thinking that someone or something is looking after her. Her husband used to take care of her; now God is. Grace thought that if she served God through church-related activities she would be rewarded in heaven later. She became very involved in her parish teaching children catechism, working at bingo, and volunteering to decorate the church before holidays. She really enjoyed the attention she received through her involvement in her church. She felt important when other parishioners asked her for advice about what to do next to organize fund-raising events like summer lawn fetes (carnival-type church picnics).

After volunteering for a number of church-related events, a priest at her parish, to whom she talked extensively after her husband's death, asked her to organize a pro-life protest that was to be held at a local Planned Parenthood. While she did not approve of abortion, she hadn't thought about it extensively until then. In organizing for the protest, she read a lot of literature from the church on abortion and was appalled that it was legal. She quickly became very active in the pro-life movement, frequently attending and organizing protests for a variety of organizations supporting this view. She sees it as her mission to save babies. She has no sympathy for women who find themselves pregnant and unmarried. She couldn't understand why anyone would not want a child God had given them. The priests at her parish describe her as strong, devout, outspoken, and driven.

Other people describe her in other ways. Her son-in-law describes Grace as self-righteous and stubborn, a religious zealot. She and her son-in-law, Nick, do not get along well. Her daughter, Hannah, married Nick a year and a half after Grace's husband (Hannah's father) died. Grace did not approve of the marriage and was quite vocal about her disapproval. Primarily she complained that Nick wasn't good enough for Hannah. He didn't earn enough money, he didn't help out around the house enough, he had too big of an ego, and so on. She was quite critical of him. According to Grace, the only thing Nick was good for was the sperm he donated to her grandson, the apple of her eye. Nick was not the only person she was critical of. Although she loved her daughter, she was judgmental of her as well, especially the way she parented. In fact, she found fault with most people with whom she interacted and either made unfavorable comments to their face or made disparaging remarks about them to others. Despite her Christian background, she was actually quite judgmental and unforgiving. Although others noticed this tendency in Grace, she did not see it in herself and instead thought of herself as kindly. Should anyone point out this contradiction, she would immediately attack that person verbally. Afterward, she would not forgive them, secretly harboring ill thoughts toward that person indefinitely.

Grace tried a number of other activities to help ease her loneliness after her husband died and her daughter got married. For example, for a time, she, and a number of other women she knew from her church, got together once a week to do scrapbooking. They would talk, have snacks, and work on their scrapbooks together. She hesitated joining the group at first because she wasn't really interested in scrapbooking but did so anyway because she thought it would be good for her to reach out to others in her loneliness. It turned out that she liked scrapbooking once she gave it a try, and even though that group has disbanded, she continues this hobby. She thinks it's important to document her life with her husband and child. In fact, her son-in-law thinks she has gone too far in her scrapbooking. It has become a passion, and she is determined to paste the hundreds of photographs she has of her family to scrap-book pages along with short descriptions of the experiences they illustrate. This passion, however, helps Grace cope with her loss and eases the pain of missing her husband.

APPLICATION QUESTIONS

Using Allport's trait theory approach, describe Grace's personality by answering the following questions.

1. Allport suggested seven criteria that demonstrate that a person is psychologically healthy. What are they? Find examples of them in the case.
2. What are central traits? Which seem to describe Grace?
3. What is functional autonomy? Find an example of propriate functional autonomy in the case.

4. What did Allport say about religious orientation? How is religious orientation related to adjustment? Does Grace have an internal or external religious orientation? Explain. What does this imply about her adjustment?

THEORY COMPARISON QUESTIONS

1. How could Bandura explain functional autonomy?
2. What would Jung say about Grace's religious orientation?

Helpful Hints

Are you having a problem answering some of the application questions for Case 31 or 32? See if the following will help you.

Allport distinguished between cardinal, central, and secondary traits. Central dispositions are key characteristics of a person. Secondary traits are more specific and less important to a personality. Cardinal traits are very pervasive, so pervasive that they intrude upon a wide range of a person's activities. Few people have cardinal traits. Allport thought that we all had five to ten central dispositions. These are the adjectives that friends would describe us as having.

Although Allport is most known for this classification system of traits, there are also other aspects to his theory; it is not just a classification system. He also discussed the proprium (Allport's term for the self), and relatedly, to functional autonomy. Functional autonomy occurs when a behavior continues even after the original motivation for it is removed. Functional autonomy has two levels: preservative and propriate. Preservative functional autonomy is more elementary and peripheral to the proprium. Behaviors that fall under this category are often habits. Propriate functional autonomy explains behaviors that are more

central to the proprium. A term similar to this is propriate striving. Propriate striving, however, does not explain motivation for a behavior as does propriate functional autonomy. Rather, it is that aspect of the self that allows us to move toward growth by moving toward long-range goals.

Allport also discussed criteria for psychological maturity. He thought that well-adjusted people:

- were motivated by conscious (as opposed to unconscious) processes (i.e., they were aware of their behavior and why they behave in the way they do).
- have an extended sense of self (i.e., they are not self-centered).
- relate warmly to others.
- accept themselves for who they are, even their faults.
- have a realistic perception of the world.
- have insight and humor.
- have a unifying philosophy of life, (i.e., a clear purpose in life).

Raymond Cattell (1905–1998)

16 Factor Theory
Why learn this theory?

Contributions

Cattell is sometimes described as the father of personality trait measurement. His goals were to use a systematic, scientific process to discover and describe the basic units of personality and to develop a reliable and valid method for measuring these basic units. Thus, his research interest was the structure of personality, but he was also interested in the predictive value of these basic units, which he called traits. He is best known for his 16 factor theory and for contributing dramatically to the understanding of personality assessment and personality measurement. He distinguished between different types of traits, including surface traits, which are clusters of observable behaviors that are similar, and source traits, which are the basic units of a person's personality and

are visible through surface traits. He likewise discussed temperament traits, which describe how a person behaves, motivational traits, which explain why a person behaves as s/he does, and ability traits, which explain how well a person can perform a behavior. In addition to making distinctions between types of traits, Cattell also distinguished between different types of intelligence, including fluid intelligence, which is independent of previous experiences, and crystallized intelligence, which is based upon past learning experiences. Despite the fact that his research, and his findings, relied heavily on the previous research of other scientists, his research was instrumental in the development of more current research on the five factor theory.

Case Study 33
Raymond Cattell

Walter is a 55-year-old minister of a conservative Southern Baptist Church. His congregation is small; fewer than 100 people attend his church, and most of those people are 50 years or older. He is concerned that his church is not growing because younger people are not joining, and he is afraid that with time it will actually die out.

Walter has always been religious, having been raised in a religious family. When he was a teenager, he received a "calling," which he describes as God telling him to become a minister. To fulfill God's will, Walter enrolled at a seminary but flunked out his first semester. He was not dismayed, however, and believed that God was guiding him to the correct path to fulfill His will. Walter enrolled in a Bible school from which he subsequently graduated. After Bible school, Walter was eventually "called" to be interviewed at the small church that he now leads.

His choice of profession is an appropriate one because Walter has a handicap that would make other, more physical, types of work difficult. Walter was born with one leg shorter than the other, and he limps quite dramatically. Walter believes that his church is just one of the many examples of God providing for him. To supplement his income as a minister, Walter also sorts small packages for a delivery service. He really does not worry too much about money because he has faith in God taking care of his needs. Occasionally, he wishes for more material possessions, but Walter also knows that he should not be concerned with such worldly goods. He struggles between worldly wants and spiritual needs.

His congregation trusts and admires Walter. Walter is good at what he does and is confident of his abilities as a minister. He is a motivational speaker with a booming voice who delivers inspirational sermons. He moves slowly and precisely because of his handicap, and these characteristics seem to have permeated the rest of his personality. He is a cautious man—he had to be cautious in his movements—and he thinks long and hard before making decisions. His decisions, like his movements, are meticulously made. He carries himself with authority.

Walter tries to fulfill not only his spiritual needs but those of his family and his congregation as well. He wonders what his responsibility is to others who are not part of his flock. He believes that although other people attend church, they will not be able to enter heaven at the Time of Redemption because they are members of the wrong church and do not have the correct beliefs. Should he tell them this? Or should he concentrate on his own following? He believes the end of the world will come soon. To him, the societal changes occurring are signs of the forthcoming end. These changes are disturbing to him. He believes they are signs of immorality and that God is most displeased with these changes.

Walter met his wife, Lillian, at the church that he heads. He was pleased that she agreed to marry him. He thought that no one would want to marry him because of his handicap. Lillian was religious, and conservative as well, so Walter and Lillian made a good match. Lillian was especially pleased to serve God by becoming a minister's wife and had no qualms about agreeing to be submissive to her husband because the Bible indicated that it was the right thing to do. She certainly was submissive to Walter. Walter was, without a doubt, the head of the family. Both Lillian and their children obeyed everything he said. His every whim was granted. That is, until recently. With his children grown and with children of their own, there has been some strife about such things as where Sunday dinner would be held or at whose house Christmas should be celebrated. These events were always held at Walter's house, but now his children want them at their houses. As head of the household, Walter believes that there should be no discussion; they should be at his house. For Walter, this is yet another example of the moral decay of society that indicates the coming of the Lord.

APPLICATION QUESTIONS

Using Cattell's trait theory approach, describe Walter's personality by answering the following questions.

1. If one considers Walter's attendance at the seminary and Bible school as attitudes (according to Cattell's definition), what would be some of the sems/sentiments that motivated those behaviors? Explain.

2. What would be some of the ergs that motivated Walter's choice of profession, according to Cattell's theory? Explain.

3. What would be some of the ergs that motivated Walter's marriage and the formation of his family, according to Cattell? Explain.

4. List some of Cattell's 16 source traits that Walter might score high on. Which might he score lower on? Explain.

5. Describe Walter's temperament traits, according to Cattell's trait approach.

6. Describe Walter's ability traits, according to Cattell's theory.

THEORY COMPARISON QUESTIONS

1. How do Fromm's character orientations compare with the traits discussed by Cattell?

2. Apply Adler's theory to Walter's behavior. How does Adler's style of life compare with the traits discussed by Cattell?

Case Study 34
Raymond Cattell

Brian is a 31-year-old veteran. He returned home from the war in Iraq a number of years ago because of a severe injury. A car bomb exploded near a checkpoint where he was standing guard. The explosion ripped his left leg to shreds, dislocated his shoulder and rendered him unconscious. The medics could not save his leg; it needed to be amputated from the knee down. But he was one of the "lucky ones." Two of his friends and fellow soldiers were killed in the blast. Upon returning home Brian was devastated by his losses, not only the loss of his leg but also the loss of his friends. He lost many friends in the war, friends who fought bravely.

Initially Brian had not planned to serve actively in combat. He joined the reservists because he needed additional income to pay for his college tuition. He was the first in his family to go to college. His grandparents immigrated legally from Mexico to the United States many years ago and worked as migrant farm workers. His parents were more settled and Brian lived in the same house his whole life. His parents never attended college, but their dream was for their children to have an even better life and thought that the only way that could happen would be for them to attend college. They could not afford to financially support Brian through college because they worked lower-paying jobs. His mother was a cook in a diner; his father worked for a landscaper. Nonetheless, they were very emotionally supportive of his college aspirations.

Brian thought it unlikely, at the time of joining the military, that he would be called up for active duty, let alone be required to serve outside the United States; he had joined the reserves before 9/11 and before the war in Iraq began. But he was called up, and he dutifully made arrangements to delay his schooling and serve his country. He had mixed feelings about this. Brian was certainly proud to be an American and to protect his country from terrorists, but he was also surprised and a little angry that he was being asked to serve in this capacity. He felt as though a trust or unspoken contract had been broken.

He thought that as a reservist he would not be called up to serve in case of war because that had been true for so long. And he was even angrier when he returned home from the war disabled. He was angry at the military. He was angry for feeling unwhole, emasculated, and inadequate. He was angry that he needed assistance to walk and complete simple tasks. He was angry he could no longer play football with friends. And he was angry because he thought that no woman would be interested in him now that he was missing a limb.

This anger led to Brian seeking relief with alcohol. Initially, Brian started drinking in the evenings to help him fall asleep. Since he returned from the war, he has been plagued with insomnia. But then the couple of beers he would have before going to bed turned into wine with dinner followed by beer throughout the evening. Brian noticed that he liked the numbness he felt in the evening. The beer and wine took the edge off the bad memories of combat and the feelings of guilt he felt about surviving the war while so many of his friends did not. This eventually led him to start drinking even earlier in the day. His parents are concerned about his drinking. It is evident to them that Brian is an alcoholic, but when they bring up the topic, he shuts them down. And because they feel so badly for their son, they are reluctant to pressure him about seeking assistance.

His childhood friends have also noticed a change in Brian since he returned from the war. Old high school girlfriends, with whom Brian kept in touch, described him as warm and caring before the war. Now he seems distant and aloof. His male friends have also noticed a change: He seems jumpy and temperamental, quiet, watchful, and cautious—a great change from when Brian was growing up with them and was energetic, stable, and bold. As a child Brian was a leader on the block. Blessed with many other children that lived in close proximity, Brian and his friends were able to get together after school and play baseball or football or tag. During long summers, it was always Brian who came up with new ideas about what to do. And many of his ideas were ambitious and daring. He and his friends built a skateboard ramp and practiced tricks on it; they put together pretend carnival shows and performed not only skateboard routines but biking tricks as well. Now though, Brian doesn't want to do anything exciting. Even when they suggest going out, like trying out a new club, Brian inevitably declines. When they visit Brian at his house, they find him difficult to talk to. He jumps at the sound of a doorbell and seems to get agitated when too many friends visit at one time. It seems as though he can't wait for them to leave. And his parents noticed that his anxiety does seem to lessen once his friends are gone. They wonder if they should ask his friends to stay away for a while in order to decrease his feelings of anxiety, but they are not sure whether it's a good idea to isolate him even more when he is withdrawing from others so much already.

APPLICATION QUESTIONS

Using Cattell's trait theory approach, describe Brian's personality by answering the following questions.

1. What is a subsidiation chain? Explain the subsidiation chain involved in this case, if one considers Brian's serving in Iraq as an attitude (according to Cattell's definition). What would be some of the sems/sentiments that motivated those behaviors? What are some ergs that motivated Brian's choice of profession? Explain.

2. Explain the subsidiation chain involved if one considers Brian's alcoholism as an attitude (according to Cattell's definition). What would be some of the sems/sentiments and ergs that motivated this behavior? Explain.

3. What is the difference between a source trait and a surface trait, according to Cattell? What are some of Brian's source traits and surface traits before and after his service in Iraq? Use evidence from the case to support your answer.

4. How could Cattell justify describing Brain's personality differently before and after his time in Iraq? Did Cattell think personality traits were stable across time?

THEORY COMPARISON QUESTIONS

1. How does Cattell's conceptualization of abnormal behavior compare to that of Horney's conceptualization?

2. Compare Cattell's ideas about the influence of biology and environment to those of McCrae and Costa.

Helpful Hints

Are you having a problem answering some of the application questions for Case 33 or 34? See if the following will help you.

The traits that Cattell discussed in his research on the structure of personality can be classified into a number of categories. Among them are dynamic traits. These are traits that are motivational in nature, that describe why a person behaves in the way that s/he does. These dynamic traits, in turn, can be further divided into subcategories: ergs, sentiments (or sems), and attitudes. *Ergs* are innate, unlearned motivational traits; *sems* are fairly general, learned motivational traits; and *attitudes* are fairly specific motivational traits.

(Note the difference in Cattell's usage of the term *attitude* versus today's usage of the term.) The relationships between the ergs, sems, and attitudes are found in subsidiation chains. The best way to determine a subsidiation chain is to keep asking the question "Why?" If you are examining a specific behavior (an attitude), ask why a person is engaging in that behavior, and the answer most likely will be a sem. Then ask why the sem is occurring, and the answer most likely will be an erg. A number of interlocking subsidiation chains, taken together, are referred to as a dynamic lattice. Note the reference in this term to the type of trait (dynamic) and an interlocking structure (a lattice).

Robert McCrae (1949–) and Paul Costa (1942–)

Five Factor Theory
Why learn this theory?

Contributions

McCrae and Costa's big five theory has been instru-mental in renewing interest in the basic structure of personality and in the understanding of basic traits. Findings from research on the big five indicate that certain characteristics cluster together, thus forming five basic traits. This is sometimes seen not as a theory but simply as a research finding. Therefore, some criti-cize the theory as being more of a model rather than a theory. These critics suggest that it is simply a way to describe personality, rather than understand it. It does not explain, for example, how personality develops or how the situation interacts with personality to form behavior. McCrae and Costa, however, have expanded the five factor model to include an explanation of how biological and other genetic factors also influence personality (e.g., by providing a biological basis for traits). They have likewise expanded their theory to

include a discussion of the influence of social and situ-ational factors on behavior and personality. Because of this, other personality psychologists see the big five as a very comprehensive theory that is, at least partially, supported by empirical findings. While the five factor model has been substantially supported by research, McCrae and Costa's five factor theory is a much newer and less researched formulation. In either case, as with any theory, it is important to take from it the most valuable, practical insights it provides. For the big five this means the renewed interest in trait theories. It also means the emphasis on personality psychology as a science, as the newer five factor theory certainly pro-vides ample opportunity for scientific discovery. Should the theory be empirically supported, it could poten-tially have a huge applicability value in the areas of occupational choice and clinical diagnosis.

Case Study 35

Robert McCrae and
Paul Costa

Eric is a beginning assistant professor of meteorology in a medium-sized university in the midwest. Sometimes he wonders how he got this far. During graduate school, he always thought that if he were going to be successful it would have to be because of his master's thesis or his dissertation or the articles he had written. He is fairly unattractive physically and has always been painfully aware of that fact. Likewise, he understands that his social skills are not the best. He did not believe that he would be able to obtain any type of job where he needed to interact with people in a face-to-face manner. He assumed that he would be rejected at the interview stage and believed that his research and writing skills would have to get him a job, one in which he did not have to interact much with people.

Eric certainly was a misfit as a graduate student. He was the lone Jewish student in the department of meteorology and was quite aware of that. Indeed, he often reminded others of it by bringing upcoming Jewish holidays, such as Yom Kippur, to their attention. He was very proud of his Jewish heritage—it was actually one of his defining characteristics—and his concern about increasing the awareness of others about the Jewish culture was certainly admirable. However, it was offset by his paranoia. He frequently felt persecuted because of his Jewishness. Any slight, real or imagined, was considered anti-Semitism. Some of these offenses, which we all experience at one time or another, were actually the result of other characteristics besides his Jewishness. For example, as a graduate student, he initially was not asked to be a teaching assistant because of his lack of social skills. The professors in his department did not believe that he could adequately fulfill the duties of the job. Eric, however, believed that he had been discriminated against because of his ethnic background.

Eric was an extremely precise researcher. His dissertation was based on a study of one storm that lasted five days. He spent two years studying the storm and another year writing up his analysis. Although it was very specific, it was an excellent piece of research, and he was able to publish it in a national journal.

Likewise, he was very exacting when he delivered his forecast for a forecasting game the meteorology students played every week. The graduate students would determine their forecasts for a period of five days, and the student who was most accurate won the contest. Eric spent a lot of time determining his prediction, but even with this frivolous activity, Eric would show some paranoia. He was concerned that the other students would use his forecast as a basis for theirs and improve on it, thereby winning the contest. Therefore, Eric was very secretive about his forecast and was among the last to post his predictions, even if he had completed them much earlier.

Eric's meticulous nature also showed itself in his sole social outlet outside of work: his fantasy baseball league. When he began playing this type of game, they were played through the mail; today they are played on computers over the Internet. In this league, players play baseball seasons with members managing the team and determining such characteristics of the game as batting lineup. Players in the league would send each other necessary information; then the player who received the information would play the baseball game and relay the results to the other members of the fantasy league. This activity—either the Internet version or the mail-in version—suited Eric well because he preferred not to interact with many other people. He rarely went out, and even though he was heterosexual, he went to great pains to avoid women. He was convinced that no woman would be interested in him because he was physically unattractive. In fact, one first-year meteorology student, who was a woman trying to get to know the other graduate students, introduced herself to him, and he responded, "I'm Eric, you don't want to know me." Eric did make a few friends during the time he was in graduate school. They were mostly other misfits like him, but these relationships took a long time to develop. Eric did not trust anyone until he knew that person for a long time. And there were many other graduate students that he did not like or did not trust. He certainly did not endear himself to many of the other graduate students with his self-deprecation and his persecution beliefs. But even other, more minor, behaviors alienated Eric from some of the other graduate students. For example, his office was located next to the department mail room, so many people would go in and out. His office mate, being a friendly sort, would often greet and talk to the other people who stopped to pick up their mail. This irritated Eric, and he would frequently comment that he was "working here!" Likewise, he would complain to his office mate about playing music on his computer; it disturbed Eric's ability to concentrate.

Some of Eric's friends tried to get him to try other activities, but they were unsuccessful. He did not want to go to any museums, sporting events, or the theater.

Eric preferred a simple, uncomplicated life. In many of his practices, he was very set in his ways. His clothing and his apartment were all utilitarian, and when something wore out, he simply replaced it with something similar. He did not have a true sense of style and really did not care whether his apartment or his outfits were aesthetically pleasing. In fact, his only piece of clothing that was frivolous or decorative was his Boston Red Sox baseball cap.

APPLICATION QUESTIONS

Using McCrae and Costa's five factor theory, describe Eric's personality by answering the following questions.

1. How can Eric's disposition be characterized? Is he neurotic or emotionally stable? Give evidence from the case to support your answer.
2. Would Eric be categorized as introverted or extraverted? Explain.
3. Based on the evidence in the case, could Eric be characterized as open or conventional? Explain.
4. Based on evidence in the case, would Eric score high or low on agreeableness? Explain.
5. Is Eric conscientious or aimless, according to the case? Explain.

THEORY COMPARISON QUESTIONS

1. Which of Horney's neurotic trends is Eric displaying? How do these trends compare with the traits of McCrae and Costa?
2. What would be some of the central dispositions of Eric, according to Allport's theory?
3. Compare the traits of Allport, Cattell, and McCrae and Costa. How are they different? How are they the same?

Case Study 36

Robert McCrea and
Paul Costa

Subira is a 20-year-old African-American living in New York City. As a struggling actor, she supports herself as a waitress at a trendy restaurant and bar in Manhattan. It is not a job that she wants to have forever; she desperately wants to break into Broadway but she earns good money in tips—a necessity in expensive New York—and she sees waitressing as an opportunity to polish her craft: When she waitresses she tries out a different role each evening. In this way she is able to practice acting while still earning money in this mundane type of job until she gets a break. The roles she plays as a waitress are very gregarious, flamboyant, and loud. Her friends find this very interesting because they describe her as shy. This contradiction is also apparent in her auditions. During auditions she is very outgoing; she is able to project energy and emotion—even heart-wrenching emotion—convincingly, but when she interacts with her friends and her boyfriend, she is much more reserved.

Although the money Subira earns as a waitress is enough to keep her housed, clothed, and fed, she wishes, as most people do, that she had more. She is slowly saving money for plastic surgery. Generally, she is self-conscious about her appearance. Even though she is only a size 6, she is concerned that she is too fat. She thinks her nose is too big and her breasts are too small. In fact, although most people think that she is beautiful, she wishes she could change the way she looks completely. She wishes she could look less African-American. Every dollar she saves to have her nose fixed and her breasts enlarged is a dollar closer to look-ing the way she thinks an actress *should* look. Subira feels especially vulnerable about her appearance during auditions when she sees that the majority of those auditioning are thinner than she is and are also White. This anxiety about her appearance has caused her boyfriend, Gordon, some concern. Gordon, who is also African-American, especially resents Subira's implication that Caucasian women are more attractive than African-American women.

Like others, Gordon also thinks that Subira is beautiful. He especially likes the way she dresses. You can tell by looking at her that she is artistic, imaginative, and unconventional. She dresses in a bohemian way, sometimes incorporating African-American style, as well as other cultures, into her wardrobe. Her interest in other cultures is also apparent in that she loves to try different types of food. One of her favorites is Ethiopian food. Other activities that Subira loves include spending time in Greenwich Village, wandering through the streets and observing the people there. These observations give her more ideas to choose from when she is developing the characters she plays. In fact, she generally tries as many new experiences as possible to help in the development of her craft and her characters. She would love to travel to see new sites and cultures firsthand but cannot afford it.

This diligence in developing her acting skills is also noted in Subira taking numerous acting classes, seminars, and workshops. She is dogged in going for auditions and has already landed a couple of smaller roles in not very well-known productions. She is determined to "make it" on Broadway, but her career pursuits sometimes interfere with her friendships and romantic relationships. Because she is so busy going to her acting classes and auditions and working at her waitressing job, she often runs late when she has to meet her friends or boyfriend. Occasionally she has not shown up for a lunch date because auditions ran long. In fact, Subira is not very punctual and occasionally forgets to show up for work, for example, when she says she will cover for someone else who cannot work that day. Friends and coworkers always forgive her though. She always comes through in a real crisis and is a loyal and caring, if somewhat tardy, friend. She is always sympathetic when friends come to her with problems or if they are short on cash. Subira helps out if she can. Her friends also like her because she is not difficult to please. When they make a suggestion about where to go out or what to do she readily agrees, unlike other actors they know, who often try to pressure them into going to certain clubs to "be seen."

APPLICATION QUESTIONS

Using McCrae and Costa's five factor theory, describe Subira's personality by answering the following questions.

1. What does McCrae and Costa mean by introversion and extraversion? Is Subira introverted or extraverted? Find examples in the case to support your answer.

2. What does McCrae and Costa mean by neuroticism? Would Subira score high or low on this dimension? Find examples in the case to support your answer.

3. What does McCrae and Costa mean by openness to experience? Would Subira score high or low on this dimension? Find examples in the case to support your answer.

4. What does McCrae and Costa mean by agreeableness? Would Subira score high or low on this dimension? Find examples in the case to support your answer.

5. What does McCrae and Costa mean by conscientiousness? Would Subira score high or low on this dimension? Find examples in the case to support your answer.

6. How could McCrae and Costa explain some of the inconsistencies in Subira's behavior (e.g., that she is often late to meet friends but not for auditions)?

THEORY COMPARISON QUESTIONS

1. Compare McCrae and Costa's thoughts about self-concept to those of Bandura and Rogers. How are they the same? How are they different?

2. Compare McCrae and Costa's five factor theory with Bandura's reciprocal determinism model.

3. Compare McCrae and Costa's conceptualization of introversion and extraversion to that of Jung.

Helpful Hints

Are you having a problem answering some of the application questions for Case 35 or 36? See if the following will help you.

McCrae and Costa suggest that personality is made up of five basic traits upon which people score in a low-to-high range. The combinations of scores make a person unique. These traits are neuroticism, extraversion/introversion, openness to experience, agreeableness, and conscientiousness. These are biologically based. McCrae and Costa's theory, however, goes beyond a classification system for identifying the structure of personality. They also have developed a theory that explains other aspects of

personality such as personality development and the influence of the environment (e.g., culture) on behavior and personality. McCrae and Costa suggest that behavior is determined by three key components: basic tendencies (which are biological and stable), characteristic adaptations (which are environmentally, culturally, and situationally determined as well as flexible), and self-concept (which is a very important characteristic adaptation). Behavior is also predicted by three peripheral components: biology (brain influences, genetics, hormones), objective biography (a person's experiences throughout their lifespan), and external influences (such as situations).

Evolutionary Psychology

Why learn this theory?

There is no doubt that evolutionary psychology is controversial, but this controversy is evidence that this theory has had a great impact on the field of psychology, including personality psychology. Whether you agree that there is support for the theory or not, it cannot be denied that this mode of thinking about behavior has influenced many areas of psychology. It is used as an explanation for sexual behaviors such as rape, why men prefer multiple sexual partners, and why women prefer monogamy. It is also used to explain nonsexual behaviors such as aggression and helping behaviors.

In essence, evolutionary psychology suggests that the same processes that allow our physical characteristics to evolve and change are also responsible for our social processes, our behaviors. Accordingly, the social behaviors that exist today do so because they are of evolutionary benefit. They have evolved because the biological bases for them have been passed on through genetic influence. For example, genes that determine neural connections or brain structure, which could control behavior, have been passed on from one generation to the next through reproduction. This type of thinking has dramatically created a renewed interest in biological bases for behavior and in the nature/nurture debate. Such questions as whether there are genes for certain personality characteristics are certainly of relevance to this theoretical school of thought.

Case Study 37
Evolutionary Psychology

Latisha is lying on one of the tables in the emergency room, thinking about how she ended up there. Jeremy, her husband, left her on the floor of their apartment in a huddle after beating her for almost a half hour. The beating itself didn't come as a surprise; she was used to Jeremy hitting her. He had been doing so for at least two years now. She saw the warning signs that he was about to "lose it" again. He had become increasingly critical over the last week. He complained about everything and blamed her for anything that went wrong or for anything he didn't like or that didn't measure up to his standards. Yesterday, he complained about her making dinner too late and that he didn't like the chicken. He even told her that she should have known that he wouldn't have liked the meal that she prepared and that she was stupid for not knowing that. The day before, Jeremy expressed his dissatisfaction with the way that the laundry was done: he said his shirts were wrinkled even though she had ironed them, that his socks and underwear were not put in the drawer correctly, and that she was lazy for not doing these things the right way. The day before that, Latisha had asked Jeremy about a credit card bill that she had opened up. He became enraged that she looked at the bill and, more importantly, that she had asked him about why it was so large. He told her it was none of her business and to keep out of his affairs. The truth was that even though Latisha asked Jeremy about their finances, he didn't provide her with any information.

Instead, he told her that she didn't understand money, so there was no reason for him to waste his time explaining it to her. In fact, Jeremy controlled their money completely. Even though Latisha worked part-time as a bank teller, she did not keep her paycheck: she never even saw it. She just handed over her paycheck to Jeremy who then gave her a small stipend for running the house and buying groceries. This financial arrangement began when they were first married. Jeremy had gotten a computer program to keep track of their finances and insisted on using it, although Latisha was reluctant and had trouble understanding and using computers. She was puzzled about this software purchase because Jeremy knew she didn't like to use computers. Although she tried to understand the software program, she just couldn't, and Jeremy didn't try to explain any of it to her except late at night when she was tired and just wanted to go to bed. She finally gave up and let him handle the finances.

This time the precursor to the attack was her talking to another man at a party they had attended. Jeremy had always been jealous, even when they were dating, but it seemed to have gotten worse since they were married. Jeremy had never wanted Latisha to meet his friends and discouraged her from having male friends of her own. He continuously accused her of watching other men and occasionally inferred that she was interested in having an affair. This evening Latisha had met an old college friend at the party and was reliving old times with him. She could immediately tell that something was wrong when she left the party with Jeremy. He was very cold to her as they left and on the car ride home. When they got home he accused her of flirting with the college friend and arranging for a rendezvous with him, and then he hit her. When she denied any sexual interest in her old friend, he became even more enraged and continued to hit and kick her until he finally left her on the floor when he stormed out of the house. Latisha knew that she was hurt and needed medical attention, but she couldn't drive herself to the hospital. She finally found enough energy to call a friend who came to pick her up and drive her to the emergency room.

As she lay in the emergency room, she also thought that she was lucky to have a friend drive her there. She had very few. She used to have a lot of friends before she was married, but now Jeremy insists on always knowing where she is and whom she is with. Moreover, he is very particular about who she is with. It seems as though, one by one, Jeremy has driven away her friends by being rude to them or by forbidding her to call and keep in contact with them. She even has very little contact with family members because Jeremy disapproves of them.

No, Latisha was not surprised about being beaten again; what surprised her was the severity of the beating this time and the threats against her life. The physician said it looked as though she had a couple of broken ribs, as well as a split lip, black eye, and assorted other bruises. Latisha has never felt this bad after a confrontation with Jeremy nor has she been this injured before. At the beginning of the relationship, Jeremy never hit her but sometimes would push her or grab her and shake her. After they were married, however, he began to slap her. Now the physical assaults were more extensive, especially since their discussions about having children. Jeremy wants Latisha to get pregnant; he wants children. Latisha, on the other hand, isn't sure she wants to have children with Jeremy. She wasn't even sure that she wanted to stay married to Jeremy, although she hadn't told him that until this evening. When Jeremy was accusing Latisha of wanting to sleep with her old college friend, Latisha lost her temper and threatened to leave Jeremy if he did not stop being so jealous. That was when the physical abuse escalated, and he told her that if she tried to leave him, he would hunt her down and kill her. Latisha also wonders if maybe she should just get pregnant and give Jeremy the baby he wants. Actually, Latisha does want to have children sometime. It was one of the reasons she got married. She thought that Jeremy's job as a store manager would provide a steady and reliable income, something that needs to be considered if a couple decides to have children. She thinks that maybe this is as good a time as any; maybe a baby would help the relationship with Jeremy.

APPLICATION QUESTIONS

Use the evolutionary psychology perspective to examine Latisha and Jeremy's behaviors by answering the following questions.

1. According to evolutionary psychology, why does Latisha want to have children? Why does Jeremy?
2. Explain why Latisha chose Jeremy as a spouse, according to evolutionary psychology.
3. Why does Jeremy control the family finances and refuse to allow Latisha access to any information about them, according to evolutionary psychology?
4. How does evolutionary psychology explain Jeremy's jealousy?
5. How does evolutionary psychology explain Jeremy's insults toward Latisha?
6. How does evolutionary psychology explain Jeremy beating his wife?

THEORY COMPARISON QUESTIONS

1. Which of Horney's neurotic trends does Jeremy display? How does the focus of Horney's theory compare with that of evolutionary psychology?
2. How could behaviorism explain Jeremy's violent behavior toward Latisha? What motivates behavior, according to behaviorists? According to evolutionary psychologists? How does behavioral motivation compare in these two theories?
3. According to Fromm's theory, what need would be met for Jeremy and Latisha by having a baby? How does this concept of fulfilling a need differ from what evolutionary psychologists would suggest as a reason for wanting to have children?

Case Study 38
Evolutionary Psychology

Dylan is on his third marriage, and that now appears to be on the rocks. His wife, Cassandra, just found out that he was having an affair with another woman. She had suspected this for some time, but her suspicions were confirmed when she got home before Dylan and listened to the messages on the answering machine. One of the messages was from his girlfriend, confirming plans to meet later that week. Usually Dylan was the first one home and listened to the messages; messages meant for Cassandra were written down by Dylan and given to her. She thought he was just being considerate by taking down the information; instead, he was making sure she didn't find out about "the other woman." Today had been atypical, however. After she had put in many long hours at her marketing job and finished a project, her boss gave her the afternoon off. This rarely happened, and she was looking forward to fixing a nice meal and having a romantic evening with Dylan. Instead, it turned into a terrible argument, ending with Cassandra throwing Dylan out of the house.

This isn't the first time a marriage ended for Dylan because he was having an affair. Both of his previous marriages ended for the same reason. During his first marriage, Dylan had had multiple affairs. His ex-wife, Whitney, knew about the affairs but accepted them because she thought that a man like Dylan needed more than one woman to satisfy him. He had always been sexually promiscuous in high school and college, so she reasoned that as long as he loved her, it didn't matter that there were other sexual partners. Dylan and Whitney had two children together, but then Dylan's time away from her became too extensive and obvious. After a while, she got tired of being the only one to care for the children, and she felt used, no longer loved. Rather, she felt that Dylan was no longer interested in her and just kept her around to care for the house and the children. So she filed for divorce.

Dylan married again and had another child with his second wife, Nicole. Nicole had no idea of Dylan's sexual past. He had explained his first divorce was due to irreconcilable differences, but then a friend told Nicole about Dylan having an affair, and she filed for divorce.

Besides this recurrent pattern of affairs and marriages, Dylan has another noticeably repetitive pattern of behavior in that all his wives share an uncanny resemblance to each other: they are all very attractive; of medium height, with a slender, athletic build; shiny, long, blond hair; and complexions that are just slightly tanned.

Dylan is attractive also, with an athletic build. Most likely, some of these similarities stem from the fact that Dylan usually meets his prospective wives at the fitness club he belongs to. A typical first date usually involves a tennis match and dinner afterward. Other dates often include going out dancing at a club. Dylan is an avid dancer and doesn't lack female attention. He is attractive, and it is well known among the members of the fitness club that he is quite wealthy, with a steady job as a vice president of a software manufacturing company.

Interestingly, although Dylan is quite sexually promiscuous, he rarely uses contraception. Even when his dates ask him to use condoms, he refuses because of decreased sensation. He never asks his dates whether they are on any type of birth control, either. He believes that if his dates, or his wives, are concerned about not getting pregnant or not contracting a sexually transmitted disease, the responsibility for prevention is theirs. Even though Dylan has had three children with his previous wives and is unconcerned about birth control, he is an uninvolved father who rarely spends time with his children.

APPLICATION QUESTIONS

Use the evolutionary psychology perspective to examine Dylan's behaviors by answering the following questions.

1. How could evolutionary psychology explain Dylan's promiscuity?

2. How could evolutionary psychology explain Dylan's sexual interest in women who all look the same, that is, blond, athletic, tanned, and so forth?

3. Why did all the women in the case study want to marry Dylan, according to evolutionary psychology?

4. How could evolutionary psychology explain why Dylan's first dates typically include a tennis match?

5. Why isn't Dylan interested in raising his own children, according to evolutionary psychology?

6. Why doesn't Dylan use birth control, according to evolutionary psychology?

7. What are some problems with the evolutionary psychology explanations noted here?

THEORY COMPARISON QUESTIONS

1. Use Freud's theory to explain Dylan's promiscuity. How does the focus of Freud's theory differ from that of evolutionary psychology?

2. How could Erikson's concepts of isolation versus intimacy apply to Dylan's relationships with women? How do the motivations for behavior in evolutionary psychology and in Erikson's theory compare?

3. How could Adler's concept of social interest apply to Dylan's relationships?

Helpful Hints

Are you having a problem answering some of the application questions for Case 37 or 38? See if the following will help you.

Evolutionary psychology is based on earlier notions that you've probably heard of: Darwin's ideas of evolution and survival of the fittest. The strongest, fastest, or smartest survive and hence are able to pass on their genes, thereby producing offspring who are also strong or fast or smart.

However, whereas Darwin used the concept of survival of the fittest to explain the evolution of physical characteristics, evolutionary psychologists use that same idea to explain the development or maintenance of social behavior. Two basic assumptions are significant in evolutionary psychology. First, we are all innately motivated to pass on our genes. Second, any behaviors that we display today are of evolutionary benefit; they help the species to survive. Thus, in attempting to explain why a certain behavior exists, ask yourself: How does this behavior contribute to the passing on of our genes, and how does the behavior contribute to the survival of the species?

Additional Theory Comparison

Multiple Explanations for
the Same Behavior

Theory Comparison Charts

Are you having trouble making distinctions between theories? Some theorists use the same terms but mean something different by them. Other theorists use different terms to refer to similar concepts; sometimes one theorist even uses different terms to mean the same thing! Use the following comparison charts to help you make distinctions.

Theory Comparison: The Structure of Personality

Theorists envisioned the structure of personality in a variety of ways. Here is a summary of their ideas:

- **Freud**—Personality is the interaction between the three systems of personality: the id, ego, and superego. Our personality is based on the outcomes of the conflicts at each of the five psychosexual stages.

- **Jung**—The ego is the center of the conscious mind. Note the difference in his use of the term versus Freud's, who suggested that the ego interacted between the id and the external world and worked on the reality principle. Jung also stated that, in addition to the conscious, there was the personal unconscious, where material is organized in clusters, and the collective unconscious that contains the archetypes. Jung likewise discussed eight personality types consisting of a combination of one of two attitudes (introverted or extraverted) and one of four functions: thinking or feeling (rational functions) or sensing or intuiting (irrational functions).

- **Erikson**—Erikson discussed the id, ego, and superego but emphasized ego functioning. However, his use of the terms differed from that of Freud. The ego, for example, was more a matter of the self than a structure that works on the reality principle. Our personality is based on the outcomes at each of the crises of the eight psychosocial stages.

- **Adler**—Personality is unified. All behavior stems from feelings of inferiority and motivates us to strive for success. How we define success varies, as does our style of life, which determines how we will strive for success.

- **Horney**—We use three neurotic trends (or basic adjustments) in order to combat basic anxiety and fulfill 10 neurotic needs: moving toward others (the compliant personality), moving against others (the aggressive personality), and moving away from others (the detached personality).

- **Fromm**—The most important component in personality is character. There are five character orientations: the receptive, hoarding, exploitative, marketing, and productive orientations.

- **Sullivan**—Personality is an energy system. Energy can exist as a tension (potential for action) or an energy transformation (action). A dynamism is an enduring energy unit.

- **Maslow**—We continually attempt to fulfill the needs of Maslow's hierarchy including physiological,

safety, esteem, love and belongingness, and actualization needs. How we do so varies from person to person and culture to culture. Our personality is based on whether, and how, we satisfy these needs.

- **Rogers**—All behavior revolves around the actualizing tendency. Either we try to actualize our organismic self (who we really are) or we fall victim to conditions of worth as we try to actualize someone else's concept of us.

- **May**—There are three modes of existence: the umwelt (physical), mitwelt (personal relationships), and eigenwelt (consciousness). Alienation is feeling separate from any of these. We are responsible for our own growth and lives. Living life according to our own terms is called authenticity. We must rediscover our selfhood in order to be authentic.

- **Kelly**—Our construct system is arranged in a hierarchical fashion.

- **Skinner**—Personality is the sum total of our conditioning history.

- **Bandura**—Behavior is a product of reciprocal determinism. Behavior is influenced by, and influences, the environment and person factors.

- **Rotter**—Personality is learned and capable of being modified because of new experiences. It is stable because of the accumulation of past experiences. Behavior in a specific situation is a function of the expectations of reinforcements and the strengths of needs these reinforcements can fulfill.

- **Allport**—Two basic units of personality are personal dispositions and the proprium. There are three levels of personal dispositions: cardinal traits, central traits, and secondary traits. The proprium consists of behaviors and traits that are most central to a person. It is a person's sense of who they really are.

- **Cattell**—Personality is a system of traits. There are 16 normal basic traits (factors). Dynamic (motivational) traits are organized in a dynamic lattice that is a series of subsidiation chains. A subsidiation chain consists of an erg, a sem (sentiment), and an attitude.

- **McCrae and Costa**—Personality is composed of five basic traits: introversion/extraversion, neuroticism/emotional stability, openness/conventionality, agreeableness, and conscientiousness.

Theory Comparison: Stages of Development

While some theorists focused on the structure of personality, others focused on the development of personality. Some wrote about both. Some theorists suggested that personality develops during early childhood and then remains fixed. Others suggested that personality develops throughout the life span. Many discussed the stages people go through as their personality develops. Here is a summary of their ideas:

- **Freud**—There are five psychosexual stages: oral, anal, phallic, latency, and genital. The libido cathects (attaches) onto an area of the body, and that, in turn, determines the stage we are in. Our experiences at each of the stages help to determine personality. Freud's focus was on early childhood, and he suggested that personality was pretty much fixed by the age of six.

- **Jung**—People progress through four stages: childhood (including anarchic, monarchic, and dualistic substages), youth, middle life, and old age. His focus was more of a life-span approach.

- **Erikson**—There are eight psychosocial stages (oral sensory, muscular anal, locomotor-genital, latency, adolescence, young adulthood, middle adulthood, and mature adulthood). His life-span approach suggested that we progress through the crisis at each of these stages as a function of social adaptation.

- **Sullivan**—Sullivan suggested seven stages or epochs: infancy, childhood, juvenile era, preadolescence, early adolescence, late adolescence, and adulthood. How we progress through these stages is determined by our interpersonal relationships.

- **May**—There are four stages of consciousness as we rediscover our selfhood: innocence, rebellion, ordinary consciousness, and creative consciousness.

Theory Comparison: Personality Types and Traits

Many theorists describe categories of personality types. The types vary among the theories, as do their causes. Some types develop because of early childhood experiences or as an effort to compensate for anxiety. Other types are determined by traits. Others describe different "types" of personalities and have a set number of categories for those personalities. Here is a summary of their ideas:

- **Freud**—Personality types are based on fixations at the psychosexual stages (e.g., oral aggressive, anal retentive, anal expulsive, and phallic).

- **Jung**—There are eight personality types based on two attitudes (introversion and extraversion) and four functions (thinking, feeling, sensing, and intuiting).

- **Adler**—We all strive for success to alleviate feelings of inferiority but how we define success varies as does our style of life, which determines how we will strive for success. Birth order also influences personality.

- **Horney**—There are three personality types: compliant, aggressive, and detached. These are characterized by the trends of moving toward others, moving against others, and moving away from others, respectively. These trends and types are influenced by the types of neurotic needs by which people are motivated.

- **Fromm**—There are five character orientations, one of which is productive (healthy). The other four are the receptive, exploitative, hoarding, and marketing orientations, all of which are unproductive (unhealthy).

- **Sullivan**—Personality is a person's interpersonal style.

- **Bowlby and Ainsworth**—Three types of attachment styles can develop depending upon early childhood attachment to caregivers. If the child develops a secure attachment to his/her parents, s/he will develop a secure attachment style that will be reflected in adult relationships. If the child does not develop a secure attachment to his/her parents, s/he can develop either an avoidant or an ambivalent attachment style that can also be reflected in adult relationships.

- **Maslow**—Maslow did not discuss personality types or traits per se but did discuss those who embrace B values and those who did not. Those who embrace B values are more likely to strive for actualization.

- **Kelly**—A person's personality is determined by the organization of their personal constructs.

- **Rotter**—People can be categorized according to whether they have an internal or external locus of control.

- **Allport**—Personality can be described through three levels of traits: cardinal, central, and secondary.

- **Cattell**—Personality can be described by assessing 16 factors.

- **McCrae and Costa**—Personality consists of five basic factors: introversion/extraversion, neuroticism/emotional stability, openness/conventionality, agreeableness, and conscientiousness.

- **Evolutionary Psychology**—Any personality types that exist today are of evolutionary benefit.

Although there is some overlap, theorists define adjustment and maladjustment in a variety of ways. They also vary in what they see as the cause of maladjustment. Here is a summary of their ideas:

- **Freud**—Well-adjusted people resolve the crisis at each psychosexual stage successfully. Unhealthy people are fixated at one of the stages due to either neglect or overindulgence.

- **Jung**—Well-adjusted people are well rounded, that is, self-realized. Unhealthy people focus too much on one aspect of their personality, ignoring other unconscious urgings.

- **Erikson**—Well-adjusted people resolve the crisis at each psychosocial stage successfully. Maladjusted people have been relatively unsuccessful in resolving the crisis.

- **Adler**—Well-adjusted people have a high level of social interest and are conscious of the behaviors they use to meet their goal of striving for success. Unhealthy people have a low level of social interest and are not conscious of their goal or the behaviors they are engaging in to meet their goal.

- **Horney**—Maladjusted people use a variety of unsuccessful behaviors to alleviate their feelings of basic anxiety, which stems from feelings of insecurity and being unloved. In order to feel loved (i.e., reduce basic anxiety), people attempt to fulfill 10 neurotic needs through three trends: moving away, moving toward, and moving against others. These trends, however, make it less likely that they will form healthy relationships. Neurotics have a glorified image of themselves. Well-adjusted people move toward realization because they have been given warmth and discipline.

- **Fromm**—Well-adjusted people use self-realization or positive freedom to connect with others. Maladjusted people express the nonproductive character orientations that are based on forming unhealthy relationships with others in an effort to connect with others.

- **Sullivan**—Well-adjusted people have healthy interpersonal styles.

- **Bowlby and Ainsworth**—Well-adjusted people have had secure attachments to their childhood caregivers that are reflected in healthy adult relationships. Insecure early childhood attachment to caregivers results in maladjustment and unhealthy relationships later in life.

- **Maslow**—Well-adjusted people have had their needs met. Maladjustment results from not having needs met.

- **Rogers**—A well-adjusted person actualizes the organismic self. Their selves are congruent (similar). Maladjustment results from a discrepancy among the selves (e.g., there is a large discrepancy between the ideal self and self-concept), most likely due to conditions of worth.

- **May**—Unhealthy people experience alienation, that is, they feel separated from either *umwelt* (physical existence), *mitwelt* (personal relationships), or *eigenwelt* (personal consciousness, i.e., oneself). Healthy people have discovered their own feelings and desires (rediscovering selfhood). They are authentic. A loss of values can also result in unhealthy individualism and unhealthy communal orientations whereas adjusted individuals develop healthy individualism and a healthy communal orientation.

- **Kelly**—Well-adjusted people are able to validate their personal constructs and make adjustments to them as necessary. Maladjusted people continue to cling to unsupported constructs. Their constructs fail the test of permeability: They are either too impermeable or too flexible.

- **Skinner**—Well-adjusted behavior is reinforced, as can be maladjusted behavior.

- **Bandura**—Maladjusted behaviors result from reciprocal determinism, that is, the interaction between the environment, person factors, and behavior.

- **Rotter**—Well-adjusted behavior moves a person closer to a goal. Maladjusted behavior does not move a person closer to a goal. Maladjusted people often have unrealistic goals.

- **Allport**—There are seven requirements for psychological health: 1. an extended sense of self, 2. relating warmly to others, 3. being emotionally secure or self-accepting, 4. a realistic perception of the environment, 5. having insight and a sense of humor, 6. a unifying philosophy of life; and 7. being motivated by conscious processes. Those that meet these requirements are well-adjusted; those that do not are maladjusted.

- **Cattell**—There are both normal and abnormal traits and both types overlap somewhat.

- **McCrae and Costa**—Maladjusted people would score high on the neurotic side of the neurotic versus emotionally stable factor. Adjusted people would score high on the emotionally stable pole.

- **Evolutionary Psychology**—Any behavior that exists today, whether it be adjusted or maladjusted, is of evolutionary benefit.

Theory Comparison: Defense Mechanisms

Many theorists describe defense mechanisms that we use to combat anxiety. A number of these concepts overlap among the theorists although they sometimes go by different names. Other defense mechanisms are unique to the theorist. Here is a summary of their ideas:

- **Freud**—Defense mechanisms distort reality to keep the unconscious from entering the conscious (e.g., denial, repression, suppression, projection, reaction formation, intellectualization).

- **Horney**—Secondary defenses are used by neurotics to maintain their idealized self-concept (e.g., cynicism, elusiveness, excessive self-control, externalization, blind spot, compartmentalization, rationalization, arbitrary rightness).

- **Adler**—Safeguarding tendencies are used to protect an inflated self-image and to maintain a neurotic lifestyle (e.g., excuses, aggression, including depreciation and accusation, withdrawal, including moving backward, standing still, and hesitating).

- **Fromm**—We reduce anxiety by utilizing three unhealthy mechanisms (authoritarianism, including masochism and sadism, destructiveness, and conformity).

- **Sullivan**—Security operations protect us from feelings of anxiety (and so develop out of the interpersonal situation). Two security operations are dissociation and selective inattention.

- **Rogers**—When we experience incongruence (inconsistencies) between the selves, we will behave in a defensive way. Two important defenses are distortion and denial.

- **Skinner**—Defensive behavior has been reinforced.

- **Evolutionary Psychology**—Defensive behavior exists because it is of evolutionary benefit.

Theory Comparison: Needs

Many theorists discuss the concept of needs. Some of the needs overlap among theorists; others are distinct to a particular theory. Here is a summary of their ideas:

- **Horney**—There are 10 neurotic needs that characterize people as they try to combat basic anxiety, including the needs for affection and approval, for a partner, to narrowly restrict one's life, for power, to exploit others, for social recognition or prestige, for personal achievement, for personal admiration, for self-sufficiency and independence, and for perfection and unassailability.

- **Fromm**—There is a distinction between animal needs (physiological needs) and human needs (existential needs). Fulfilling existential needs helps us to reunite with nature, and includes the needs for effectiveness, relatedness, transcendence, rootedness, sense of identity, frame of orientation, unity, and excitation and stimulation.

- **Sullivan**—There is a distinction between general needs that can be either biological or interpersonal (such as the need for tenderness) and zonal needs that focus on areas of the body.

- **Bowlby and Ainsworth**—Children have a need for a warm, responsive caregiver in order to develop a secure attachment that will serve as a model for future adult relationships.

- **Maslow**—Needs are arranged on a hierarchy and include physiological, safety, love and belongingness, esteem, and actualization needs. Lower level needs must be met before the higher level needs.

- **Rogers**—Maintenance needs (the need to keep things the same) and enhancement needs (the need for change, growth, and development) seem contradictory but are not. We also have needs for positive regard and self regard.

- **Rotter**—Needs motivate behaviors that move us toward our goals. They have three components: need potential, freedom of movement, and need values. There are six basic categories of needs, including the needs for recognition or status, dominance, independence, protection or dependency, love and affection, and physical comfort.

- **Evolutionary Psychology**—We have the need to pass on our genes.

Theory Comparison: The Self

Many theorists discuss the self, and many discuss different aspects of the self as well as different ideas about what the self is. Here is a summary of their ideas:

- **Jung**—The self archetype unites all other archetypes and all aspects of our personalities through the process of self-realization.

- **Erikson**—Erikson did not discuss the self, per se, but did discuss the similar concept of identity that develops in the fifth of his eight psychosocial stages. Identity is a sense of knowing who we truly are and develops when there is a positive resolution of the identity versus role confusion crisis.

- **Horney**—Horney distinguished between the real self (who we actually are) and the idealized self (who we think we should be). Neurotics have a glorified image of themselves.

- **Sullivan**—The self system is a device that protects us from anxiety. Anxiety develops out of the interpersonal situation. Two basic goals of the self system are satisfaction (fulfilling biological needs) and security (fulfilling social needs).

- **Rogers**—The organismic self includes all aspects of the self, even those we are not aware of.

Self-concept is our perception of our self, which can be accurate or inaccurate. The ideal self is who we would like to be. The selves are fairly consistent in a well-adjusted person.

- **May**—We need to rediscover our selfhood (i.e., our own feelings, wants, etc.). There are four stages of consciousness as we rediscover our selfhood: innocence, rebellion, ordinary consciousness, and creative consciousness.

- **Bandura**—The self system is a set of cognitive structures that encourage consistent behavior. It allows us to engage in self-regulation, the three steps of which are self-observation, self-judgment, and self-evaluation. Self-efficacy is a person factor that is our belief in whether we can or cannot successfully perform a behavior.

- **Allport**—The proprium consists of behaviors and traits that are key, central, or important to a person. It is our sense of our "true" self.

- **McCrae and Costa**—Self-concept is a characteristic adaptation; it can fluctuate depending on the circumstances. Although it is relatively accurate, there is room for distortion.

Theory Comparison: Actualization

Although the term actualization is often associated with Maslow, other theorists also used the term or referred to similar concepts utilizing different terminology. Here is a summary of their ideas:

- **Jung**—Jung's concept of self-realization is similar to self-actualization. In striving toward self-realization, we strive to develop and integrate all aspects of our personality.

- **Adler**—The concept of striving for success or superiority is similar, but not identical, to that of actualization in that they both revolve around challenges and endeavors. Adler also took a holistic view of the person as humanists (who typically discuss actualization) do.

- **Fromm**—Fromm did not discuss actualization, per se, but his theory is somewhat humanistic; he did discuss concepts similar to actualization. Most notable is positive freedom, which allows spontaneity and complete expression of potential. Love and work are the two primary components of positive freedom.

- **Maslow**—Actualization is reserved for only a few people who embrace B values. It is a matter of working toward one's own full potential.

- **Rogers**—The actualization tendency is different from self-actualization and from the need to actualize. Self-actualization is the tendency to actualize the perceived self (which might or might not be an accurate self-concept) and is a subsystem of the (more general) actualization tendency. The need to actualize is the need for change, growth, and to achieve more. Thus, while we all have the need to actualize, some of us actualize our real selves. Others actualize an inaccurate version of themselves.

- **May**—Similar to Rogers' thoughts on actualizing an accurate perceived self, May thought it was important for people to rediscover their self-hood. May's concept of the three modes of being-in-the-world (*umwelt, mitwelt, eigenwelt*) is similar to Jung's self-realization because it involves the integration of the whole person/personality.

- **Allport**—Allport did not discuss actualization, per se, but did suggest that the psychologically healthy person needs to adjust to their environment and to grow.

Case Study 39

Every time Sarah calls her mother Myra, the conversation is very similar. Myra essentially describes that she is in the midst of cleaning her house. Sarah is well acquainted with this behavior. Myra takes great pride in the appearance of her house and yard and loves it when someone compliments either. As a child, Sarah remembers Myra continuously cleaning on weekends when she was not working outside her home. She would clean the entire house room by room, making beds, dusting furniture and woodwork, shaking out rugs. The entire process took a day and a half. When the family was expecting company during the holidays, it was assumed that the house would be cleaned twice, once during the regular weekly cleaning and once the day the company was visiting. When company visited, the living room furniture, which was normally covered with plastic, was uncovered, and the sheet that was laid down on the rug in the living room entrance was picked up and put away. The plastics and the sheet helped to maintain the furniture and rug far beyond the usual life span. This helped the family to save money. Once a year, spring cleaning took place. Everyone in the family, except Myra, dreaded this process. During this event, closets were cleaned out and washed. Hardwood floors were washed and waxed. Woodwork and rugs were washed. Furniture was polished. Curtains were washed and rehung. All the dishes were taken out of the cupboards and washed, and the cupboards were also washed. Then everything was returned to its place. Everything had a place in Myra's house, and she frequently would become angry if there were too many things out of place. "Family conferences" would be called to discuss ways to help keep the house clean and how hard Myra worked at keeping the house clean while everyone else did so little. Actually, this was a common theme. Myra frequently portrayed herself as a martyr who did so much for others and asked so little for herself. She sees herself as continuously doing for others, when in reality she usually told others what to do.

The yard is also very tidy. The grass is beautifully trimmed and resembles a rug. It is often mowed, even though it does not appear to need it. The garden is well tended; it would be difficult to find a single weed in it. Once when a neighbor cut his grass without a catcher attached to the lawn mower and grass went flying into her garden, Myra threw a fit. After that, she did not talk to the neighbor for two years.

Now that Myra is retired, the cleaning continues. She always thought that it was her job to care for the house. She was always the one who oversaw the cleaning, although her children or her husband would help. Myra's mother always took care of their house and thought that it was the woman's responsibility to do so.

Myra learned how to clean "correctly" from her mother. Both Myra's parents believed in physical punishment, and Myra and her brother were hit if they did something wrong. Myra was punished if she did not clean something thoroughly enough.

Myra made sure that her family saved money. Some of the activities that she engaged in to save money revolved around cleaning issues, such as the plastic and sheets used to save the furniture and rugs, but Myra saved money in various other ways as well. Sometimes Myra would wash and reuse aluminum foil. Leftovers were eaten even if they were unappetizing and no one felt like eating them. There was always a concern for money even though the family really was not poor nor lacking in any of the essentials. This was so extreme that Myra would become agitated when someone borrowed 50 cents for a soda and did not return it. Myra would tell stories about relatives who would accept invitations to her house but did not return the invitations. The primary complaint about this was that she was tired of spending money on these occasions without ever getting something in return.

In fact, Myra displayed a disturbing pattern of establishing relationships and then ending them by being rude. She would have an intense relationship with someone she had just started a friendship with, often having that person over for lavish meals and then complaining about some aspect of that person's personality to Sarah. Myra would sometimes even criticize people to their faces, or she would just stop calling them. Often, these complaints revolved around the idea that Myra was superior to them in some way. For example, someone was too loud and Myra wasn't; Myra's house was cleaner; Myra's cooking was better; and so on. When these people no longer wanted to interact with her, Myra did not understand why.

The family very rarely spent money on anything except the necessities even though they were middle class and could afford it. Thus, they rarely engaged in activities such as going to the movies, and the children felt as though asking for a new toy was totally unreasonable.

Although Myra is still healthy and she could participate in a number of other productive activities, such as volunteer work, she does not, preferring to spend all her time and energy working on her house and yard. When she visits her grown children, she is dismayed by how messy their homes are, and she begins to clean them. She frequently complains about how other people don't know how to clean anymore and that her neighbors don't take care of their property as well as she does.

APPLICATION QUESTIONS

1. Which personality type does Myra display, according to Freudian theory? Provide evidence for your answer. What caused it?

2. Why does Myra feel that cleaning the house is her responsibility? How would Jungian theory explain Myra adopting this traditional role?

3. How could radical behaviorism explain Myra's cleaning behavior? Find examples of reinforcement or punishment that might have influenced Myra's cleaning behavior.

4. How could Bandura's social cognitive theory explain Myra's traditionally feminine cleaning behavior?

5. Which of Horney's needs motivate Myra? Which of Horney's neurotic trends does Myra demonstrate? Provide evidence for your answer.

6. How could Horney's theory explain the discrepancy between Myra's idealized versus real image of herself?

7. How could Fromm's theory describe Myra's mechanism of interpersonal relatedness? What character type best describes Myra, according to his theory?

8. Explain whether Myra would score high or low on each of McCrae and Costa's Big Five dimensions. Provide evidence for your answer.

Case Study 40

Peter has a dilemma. His work as a letter carrier is not fulfilling and is increasingly annoying and troublesome. He started this job just over three years ago. Peter has two bachelor's degrees and a master's degree. He retrained a number of times after he relocated to marry his wife, who was an established professional. He moved to a rural town of only 4,000 people where even general labor types of jobs are scarce. The nearest city, where he could attain professional work, is two hours away, and, because Peter has a wife and three small children, he is reluctant to seek employment that far away. It would either mean a four-hour commute daily or living away from his family for part of the week. Peter has been trying to find more suitable work within the post office but has been unsuccessful because many of the supervisory jobs are attained through politics rather than ability. Most recently, he was not promoted into a supervisory position at the post office where he has been working because a coworker was promoted instead. She deserved the position because she often filled in when the last supervisor was off work, but Peter could not help but feel resentful considering he interviewed very well, did his job well, and fulfilled the requirements of the position. In particular, he felt that his life experience before the post office was more valuable than additional years doing the same postal work. He is now considering quitting his job and staying home with his three young children.

As he considers this possibility, he realizes that his letter carrier job has actually been a strain on the family. Although he does bring in quite a good income, his hours change weekly and sometimes daily; he is constantly on call, so often he gets called in to work in the early morning without any notice. He also is the person to fill in for the other letter carriers when they are on vacation or sick. What this means is that he usually works when most people have time off, that is, Saturdays and summers. This is especially annoying to his wife who is a college history professor and has weekends and summers off, too. The first year he worked as a letter carrier, Peter figured out that his wife potentially has fifteen weeks off a year when she could occasionally travel or engage in other family activities. Peter was unable to take any time off at all with her because he was filling in for the other carriers. So one positive aspect of quitting his job is the possibility of spending more time with his family. Peter feels as though he has been missing out on a lot in his children's lives because he has been working so much. Certainly, staying home with the children would mean less day care for them and a smoother running home. Good dinners could be on the table, and the laundry could get done. His wife continuously complains about what a mess the house is and how much she has compromised so he could continue his job. On the other hand, quitting his job could make him feel like a failure. Although Peter is liberal and believes in equality between men and women, he still feels as though a good part of his identity comes from his job and how much money he earns. His wife does earn enough money to support their family comfortably: they could certainly pay their bills and afford to take an occasional vacation. Nevertheless, Peter is uncomfortable fulfilling the traditional female role of staying home and taking care of the kids and house. What will he tell someone he meets for the first time at a party and they ask him what he does for a living? After all, five years ago when he was unemployed and staying home with his firstborn, he took some ribbing from some of his friends for this activity. As he is considering what he should do, he is rethinking his ideas of what it means to be successful and what it means to be a man and a father.

APPLICATION QUESTIONS

1. How could Freudian theory explain Peter's behavior of wanting to be the breadwinner?

2. How could Jungian theory explain Peter's urge to quit his job and stay home with his family? How could Jung explain Peter's urge to continue working outside the home and earn money for his family?

3. How could Jung's concept of self-realization apply to this example?

4. How is Jung's concept of self-realization similar to Rogers' and Maslow's concepts of self-actualization? Is Peter showing signs of self-actualization, according to Rogers? According to Maslow? Explain.

5. How could Kelly's personal construct theory explain Peter's behavior?

6. How could radical behaviorism explain Peter's behavior? How could reinforcement or punishment have influenced Peter's wanting to be the breadwinner? Peter's wanting to quit his job?

7. Use May's concept of alienation to explain Peter's confusion about what it means to be a man and father and about his current employment situation.

Case Study 41

Glenn is a family historian of sorts. His hobby is to document the stories of his family by typing them into his computer and then to distribute them to interested family members. Currently, he is writing down stories relevant to his grandfather, Jason. As he thinks about them and writes about them, he begins to understand why his grandfather seemed so distant and aloof even though Glenn, as a child, expressed love toward him. Glenn found out a lot about his grandfather when he attended his grandfather's wake a few years back. His odd behaviors make a lot more sense to him now considering what Jason's relatives and friends said about him.

Jason was born in eastern Colorado in the 1920s just before the Great Depression of 1929, the third of four brothers, to a stay-at-home mother and a father who could be considered a farmer and cowboy, both of German-American descent. Jason's family was poor during his childhood, and their home was so small that in all except the worst weather, he was required to sleep on the front porch. Some nights it was so cold on the porch that he would wake up to a light dusting of snow on his blankets. Food was not always plentiful. Glenn remembers that his grandfather sometimes joked that on a farm, selling crops came first, then came feeding the livestock, then came feeding the children. He was only half joking really. Christmas, of course, was sparse for the children and so were new clothes. When Jason needed clothes as a small child, his mother would sew them, sometimes using burlap bags as material.

Although the family was poor, they shared what they could with others who were less fortunate than they were. When Glenn was a child his grandfather told him that strangers would stop by their house during the Depression hoping for a meal. His mother would then add another cup of water to the soup pot and give a bowl to the stranger along with a piece of bread. Jason thought that was odd at the time and couldn't imagine strangers just stopping by his house asking for a meal.

On a farm, children are expected to help with various chores, and Jason helped sell vegetables such as beets and squash from their produce truck. Jason's family also had cows, and it was Jason's and his brothers' job to sell and deliver milk from a milk truck. They would combine the watery milk of some breeds of cows with the creamier milk of other breeds to make a good product and to ensure that none of his customers was cheated. He and his whole family took pride in their work.

Glenn found out from his great-uncle that Jason had a close relationship with his mother, and that he nursed until he was three years old—until his two older brothers laughed at him. He stopped nursing because he did not want to be made fun of. Jason had a somewhat distant relationship with his father though, who was fairly uninvolved with his children. Jason's parents seemed to have a good relationship, however. They had met at a county fair when they were doing a show in which they did a kind of square dancing with horses. Jason's mother's usual partner got sick, and she was paired with his father (to be). Jason's parents married when his mother was only 16; his father was 28. They remained married for the rest of their lives. His mother had an eighth grade education; his father had a third grade education.

Over the years, Glenn found out from some of Jason's childhood friends that when Jason was a teenager, at the beginning of World War II, he went to Denver with these friends to sign up with the army. Because he was not 18 yet, Jason had to get his parent's permission to join the army, which his father gave. Although he finished high school, Jason did not wait for his graduation ceremony. He was anxious to leave Colorado and to begin his own life. He had hopes of living a life that was more comfortable and sophisticated than the life he lived as a child. After completing his high school requirements, he immediately reported for duty in the army. Jason was stationed on what could be considered the front lines of World War II, but he never had to actively battle the enemy. This was probably best considering that when he was a teenager, he went on a Sunday school hunting trip and used his father's gun to shoot his first—and last—rabbit. The animal was completely obliterated, and the experience disturbed him. Although Jason never stated it, he probably joined the army because of peer pressure and because of the idea that "that was what real men did." Glenn remembers that it had always been important to his grandfather that he be thought of as a real man, and Jason perceived himself as rugged-looking even though he was actually fairly short and not very muscular.

After Jason finished his military service, he went back to Colorado only once, when his father was sick and dying of cancer. Jason spent some time in San Francisco with his friends and worked for an airline company washing airplanes. After a short time, Jason decided to enroll for another stint in the army. After this second tour of duty, Jason left the army and attended college on the G.I. Bill. He majored in accounting, and although his academic record was not outstanding, he completed his bachelor's degree in just over three years by taking the maximum number of credits during the regular semester and by attending summer school. He supported himself with various temporary jobs such as washing dishes.

While attending college, Jason met the woman who became his wife. They married after a brief courtship and had three children. Jason worked at Westinghouse in Buffalo to support his new wife, but a recession caused him to be laid off. Throughout his life, economics influenced him, and this particular time was no different. Jason again decided to enlist in the army and attended officer's training school, which was possible for him because he had his college degree. Glenn understood that the army offered Jason some financial security.

Glenn knew from his mother, Jason's daughter, that Jason was not very involved in the raising of his children because of his position in the army. He worked long hours and often spent time on base after work at the officer's club to wind down.

During this time, Jason became increasingly distant from his family. He became more isolated from them and more involved in his work. Even his social life consisted primarily of going out with other men with whom he worked, rather than going on family outings or dates with his wife. Even when he was with his family on weekends, Jason spent time with his friends when his wife was shopping at the grocery store. He became interested in art, music, and fine food, and at any one time he subscribed to as many as 10 magazines on these topics. Jason became an increasingly cultured person, growing to appreciate the better things in life that he never had as a child. He encouraged his wife, Glenn's grandmother, to become involved in the officer's wives club but she did not enjoy the experience. This emotional distance between Jason and his family, his wife in particular, came to a pinnacle when she decided to stop having sex with him. The only reason Glenn knew this was because, as a teenager, Glenn had overheard a conversation between his grandmother and his mother about this. He wasn't sure how the conversation began but as soon as he was discovered, it ended. It seemed to be a family secret.

Years later Glenn found out more about the conversation. According to Glenn's mother, her mother, Jason's wife, later found out that he had been having homosexual relationships with various men. When confronted, Jason claimed to have been faithful to his wife. He believed that he never committed adultery because he did not have intercourse with another woman and that he did not start his homosexual activities until after his wife "cut him off." Jason did not feel guilty about his extramarital affairs. Rather, he felt victimized because his wife wouldn't have sex with him, and he claimed that the homosexual acts were nothing more than working out in the gym. His wife never divorced him, however.

Although Jason had some contact with his children after they were grown, his relationships with them were distant. He seemed to continue to have homosexual experiences until his death, but he did not have a regular partner. He never expressed regrets about anything, but he did feel closer to his past than to his present or future. An example of this is that he attended many army reunions throughout the year but rarely visited his children or grandchildren.

APPLICATION QUESTIONS

1. How could Jason's homosexuality be explained from a Freudian perspective?

2. What was Jason's goal in life, according to Adler's theory? Did he experience feelings of inferiority that influenced his life? Provide examples. How did he strive for success? Explain.

3. How could Horney's theory explain the difference in Jason's idealized versus real image of himself?

4. How would Sullivan's interpersonal personality theory explain Jason's lack of close relationships, especially with his wife and children?

5. According to Bowlby and Ainsworth, what type of adult attachment style does Jason have? Explain.

6. According to Maslow, which needs in the hierarchy were met for Jason? Which were not?

7. Point out examples of Rogers' conditions of worth in Jason's life.

8. Point out examples of Skinner's behaviorism throughout Jason's life. Describe the reinforcers and punishments and the specific behaviors they encouraged or discouraged, respectively.

9. Use Rotter's concept of expectancy to explain Jason's repeated choices to join the military.

10. Find an example of Bandura's fortuitous events that influenced Jason's behavior. How was his behavior influenced?

11. How could Kelly's theory explain the inconsistency between Jason's being homosexual and also wanting to be perceived as a "real man"?[*]

---

[*] Author's note: This does not imply that gay men are not real men, but rather reflects the common stereotype that "real men" are heterosexual.

Case Study 42

Patrick was born to an Irish-American family that was about to become affluent. His mother was a nurse; his father was an "up and coming" lawyer who was already making six figures in the middle 1970s. Patrick grew up in a beautiful house with his brother. His family also occasionally took in Patrick's friends who were having hard times. For example, one friend stayed with their family for a year when the friend's family moved during his last year in high school and the friend did not want to move with his parents to another school.

Although Patrick's family seemed to be living the American Dream, all was not well. His father was an alcoholic; the most likely cause of this was the pressure he was under at work and the long hours he spent there because of it. His drinking made him abusive; he would sometimes get into fights at bars. He beat his wife.

Although Patrick was not physically abused, he was scared for himself and his mother on these occasions. His father quit drinking when Patrick was five or six years old. Patrick's father was an athlete—a boxer who was also a golfer. He also encouraged athletics in his sons. Patrick's older brother was tall, gangly, and not very coordinated. Their father was embarrassed by his older son's clumsiness and would comment that this boy couldn't possibly be his biological son. Patrick heard these comments to his brother and was secretly afraid that he would hear similar comments about himself. Patrick's father was very competitive, and Patrick became that way, too. Patrick wanted his father's approval and tried to get it by conforming to his father's wishes. Fortunately for Patrick, playing sports came easy.

But school was not as easy for him, and academically, Patrick was not as competitive, at least initially. Patrick went to public school and was held back in the first grade, most likely because he started kindergarten at the age of five instead of six. He was a young five when he started, as his birthday was in the middle of August, and he probably was not developmentally ready to start school at that time. His parents hadn't considered this and instead decided that smaller classes might be better for him, so they sent him to an elite private school. He attended the private school for three years, and his academic performance improved as he matured and caught up with the other children. After three years, however, Patrick wanted to attend school with his neighborhood friends, and he asked his parents to let him go back to the public school. His parents granted this request, and Patrick earned good grades, mostly As and Bs, just as he did at the private school, because he wanted to continue to attend school with his friends. He was witty—the class clown—and everyone liked him, but his popularity and competitiveness in sports hid insecurity. He was concerned that he would not be able to live up to his father's standards. His initial failure in school and his father's critical nature left him unsure of himself, despite continued success.

In junior and senior high schools, Patrick continued to excel academically, socially, and athletically. He did weight training in the seventh and eighth grades, before it was popular. He was captain of the football team at his large, city high school. He also played basketball but quit that sport because he realized that he would not get a lot of playing time. Patrick liked attention and his antics in class along with his sports participation provided a lot of it. He received this attention not just from his peers but from his teachers as well. Patrick could get away with things other children could not. For example, he would often come to school late because he had stopped by a bakery on the way in. He would buy éclairs that were on sale and ask his teachers to store them for him. Then, at lunchtime, he would resell the éclairs at a profit. He got away with these schemes because his grades were good, he was an athlete, and he was charming. His superior record earned Patrick acceptance into an exclusive college.

Everything seemed to be going easily for Patrick. His acceptance into college was the next step of reaching his life's goal of becoming a lawyer like his father and working in his father's law firm. But Patrick almost flunked out of college in his freshman year. Because everything came easily for him in grade school and high school, and because he was able to charm everyone then, he thought he could do the same in college. Being away from home for the first time allowed him his first taste of freedom, and Patrick partied too much; he drank too much beer and smoked too much pot. He found himself failing his courses, especially freshman English. Patrick approached the English professor and asked her what he could do to improve his grade. She suggested extra credit work, which he completed. The extra credit was not enough, however, and he failed the course. For once Patrick could not charm himself out of trouble. His performances in his other courses were similar, and he was placed on academic probation. To make matters worse, his girlfriend, whom he started dating in high school, broke up with him. She told him he was becoming a jerk with all his partying.

Finding his life, and his dream of becoming a lawyer, crashing around him, Patrick straightened up. He quit smoking pot, drank less, did extra academic work, and improved his writing. Eventually, he was able to convince his girlfriend to come back. He maintained superior academic performance for the rest of his college career and applied for an exclusive internship with a state senator. Although he was a talented young student, he was most likely offered this internship through the influence of his father, who had political connections. With his education and internship completed, Patrick applied to the law school from which his father had graduated. He was accepted but wondered whether his acceptance was based on his own merit or whether his father helped to get him in. After law school, Patrick applied for a position in his father's law firm, which he was offered. A few years later, Patrick applied for a partnership in the firm, which he also earned. Patrick continued to have nagging doubts about whether his own performance earned his positions or whether his father helped him get his positions. He finally confronted his father, who replied that he had no influence on Patrick's getting the initial position with the firm or getting the partnership, although he did help with the internship. His father stated that Patrick went through the same hiring practices as everyone else and that he had excluded himself from the decision-making process when Patrick was applying for his positions. Patrick was finally convinced that he had earned his partnership on his own.

While in law school, Patrick married his high school sweetheart, and they had three children. He is a devoted family man who describes his children as "wonderful and beautiful." He plays with them often, and his wife sometimes describes him as her fourth child. He and his family live in a house next to the one he grew up in, and he enjoys attending functions at the school that he attended and that his children now attend. He is also active in the Congregational Church as an elder, a kind of church trustee.

APPLICATION QUESTIONS

1. Which of Erikson's stages did Patrick successfully complete? Which were not completed successfully? Explain.

2. According to Adler's theory, did Patrick experience feelings of inferiority? Provide evidence for your answer. How did these feelings influence his behavior?

3. Which of Fromm's existential needs are met for Patrick? Explain.

4. According to Bowlby and Ainsworth, what type of childhood attachment style did Patrick develop? Explain.

5. Which of Maslow's needs were fulfilled for Patrick? Which were not? Did the fulfillment of these needs change at any time in Patrick's life? Could Patrick be perceived as self-actualized, according to Maslow's theory? Explain.

6. Find an example of Rogers' conditions of worth in the case study.

7. Find examples of Skinner's radical behaviorism in the case study. How did reinforcement or punishment influence Patrick's behavior? Specify the reinforcers and/or punishments.

8. How could Rotter's concept of locus of control explain Patrick's insecurity about earning various positions (e.g., college internship, partnership in law firm) through his performance (e.g., grades or work quality) or through his father's influence?

Case Study 43

Roger, at the age of 73, is in the process of examining his life. He is trying to determine whether he lived a life that was worthwhile. In the course of his examination, Roger contemplates the various stages of his life.

He was always a superior student, even as a child in grade school, especially in reading. In early grade school, however, he was not a popular child; he had very few friends. His concern with doing well in school did not endear him with his classmates, who were less concerned with grades and more concerned with friendships and sports. He was also somewhat heavy, which hindered his athletic ability.

Roger experienced his pre-puberty growth spurt earlier than the other boys in his class did, so he was taller than the other boys during sixth, seventh, and eighth grades. This height increase slimmed Roger down; his weight stayed pretty much the same even though his height increased. Likewise, his height and strength now gave him an advantage in sports. In turn, excelling in sports made him popular in school. During high school, the other boys also grew, caught up, and even surpassed Roger's height. Because Roger experienced an early growth spurt, he also stopped growing sooner than the other boys did. In high school, he found himself to be below average in height. Nevertheless, Roger's increased contact with fellow students sharpened his social skills, and his popularity continued throughout high school and college, where Roger continued to be a superior student and a very good athlete. Now his success in sports was due to skill and intelligence, rather than strength.

Although Roger could now easily make friends and maintained many same-sex friendships, he initially had less success at the love task, partly because he felt uncomfortable with being Jewish in a predominantly Christian area. Although he dated, he did not establish any long-term relationships with women until college. During college, he met Anita and eventually they were engaged. However, Anita later fell in love with another man and broke off the engagement. Although Roger tried to salvage the relationship, it was hopeless. It was six years before Roger formed another long-term relationship and told another woman that he loved her. Jackie became his wife, and they were married for more than 40 years. Like all marriages, Jackie and Roger's occasionally had some difficult times, but Roger seemed to have found his soul mate in Jackie. They had three children: one boy and two girls.

During college, Roger chose his major and his career. In college, he majored in English because he had always loved to read. He then went on to graduate school, where he earned a Ph.D. in English. After a few temporary instructor positions with colleges, he landed a tenure-track position as an assistant professor of English at a small teaching college where he stayed for the rest of his teaching career. He was especially glad to have gotten a permanent position because it was stressful not knowing whether he would have a job the following year. The time he spent job hunting took away from the time he wanted to do other things as a professor: improve lectures, advise students, publish. While at this long-term position, he eventually earned tenure and was promoted to associate, and then to full professor. His most rewarding experiences as a teacher included encouraging young writers. While teaching, he was also able to do some writing. He acquired a contract with a publisher to write fiction, and he published a number of science fiction novels. Writing really was his love because it allowed him to be creative. Many of his novels expressed a moral concern for the future that began with the birth of his first child. Although his novels have sold well and are respected, Roger continues to try to improve his writing and wishes he could do better. Interestingly, some of his colleagues discouraged Roger from his writing. They did not publish and suggested that he should take it easy now that Roger was tenured and a full professor. Roger disagreed with this philosophy and instead believed that even full professors should continue to publish and grow.

He retired from teaching five years ago but not from writing. Roger now travels with his wife, visiting his children and grandchildren, and seeing places he has not seen before. Along with his writing, the discovery of new places and the appreciation of the beauty in these new places keeps Roger satisfied.

APPLICATION QUESTIONS

1. Use Erikson's psychosocial stages of development (especially the fourth through the eighth) to analyze Roger's life.

2. Which dynamisms had to have been fused in order for Roger to establish a mature love relationship with his wife, Jackie, according to Sullivan?

3. What type of adult attachment style does Roger have, according to Bowlby and Ainsworth? Explain.

4. How could Fromm's theory explain Roger's traveling and his visiting his children and grandchildren?

5. Find an example of how Carl Rogers' perceived self is different than his organismic self, according to Rogers' person-centered theory.

6. Roger had a different view than his colleagues did about how much work he should do after he was tenured and promoted to full professor. How could Kelly's theory explain this difference in views?

7. Using Cattell's concept of a dynamic lattice, describe the subsidiation chain involved in Roger studying English in college and graduate school. What are the ergs, sems, and attitudes involved?

8. May described four types of love. Which type of love best illustrates Roger's relationship with Jackie?

TO THE OWNER OF THIS BOOK:

I hope that you have found *Personality Theories Workbook*, Fifth Edition useful.
So that this book can be improved in a future edition, would you take the time to complete this sheet and return it? Thank you.

School and address:_____

Department: _____

Instructor's name:_____

1. What I like most about this book is:_____

   _____

   _____

2. What I like least about this book is:_____

   _____

   _____

3. My general reaction to this book is:_____

   _____

4. The name of the course in which I used this book is:_____

   _____

5. Were all of the chapters of the book assigned for you to read?_____

   If not, which ones weren't?_____

6. In the space below or on a separate sheet of paper, please write specific suggestions for improving this book and anything else you'd care to share about your experience in using this book._____

   _____

   _____

   _____

FOLD HERE

WADSWORTH
CENGAGE Learning

NO POSTAGE
NECESSARY
IF MAILED
IN THE
UNITED STATES

BUSINESS REPLY MAIL
FIRST-CLASS MAIL   PERMIT NO. 34   BELMONT CA

POSTAGE WILL BE PAID BY ADDRESSEE

Attn: *Timothy Matray, Acquisitions Editor*

Psychology

Wadsworth | Cengage Learning

20 Davis Drive

Belmont, CA 94002

FOLD HERE

OPTIONAL:

Your name:_____   Date:_____

May we quote you, either in promotion for *Personality Theories Workbook*, Fifth Edition or in future publishing ventures?

Yes:_____   No: _____

Sincerely yours,

Donna Ashcraft